The Legacy of
MORMON
FURNITURE

The Legacy of

MORMON FURNITURE

The Mormon Material Culture, Undergirded by Faith, Commitment, and Craftsmanship

by

MARILYN CONOVER BARKER

photographs by

SCOTT PETERSON

SALT LAKE CITY

Dedicated to my family—past, present, and future.

FIRST EDITION

98 97 96 95 5 4 3 2 1

This is a Peregrine Smith Book, published by
Gibbs Smith, Publisher
P. O. Box 667
Layton, Utah 84041

Design and composition by Sandy Bell
Edited by Caroll Shreeve
Printed and bound in China

JACKET (FRONT)
Architectural detail from the Beehive House
Ralph Ramsay, designer of furniture, sculptor,
   and carver of early Mormon symbols
Collection of LDS Church, Beehive House

JACKET (BACK)
Cupboard, made 1874
Ralph Ramsay
Pine, stripped of graining
82 x 20 x 43½ in.
Collection of Ralph Ramsay Home

JACKET FLAP
Public Works Stamp
Collection of LDS Church, Lagoon Corporation

FRONTISPIECE
Double Lounge
Anders Swenson
Pine, stained with oxides
31 x 23 x 80 in.
Collection of grandson Frank Swenson

OPPOSITE TITLE PAGE
The family room of the Dr. & Mrs. E. Ute
Knowlton home is furnished from their Mormon
pioneer collection.

THIS PAGE
The Salt Lake City law office of attorney Richard
Blanck is furnished with Mormon pioneer
furniture from the family's collection.

Library of Congress Cataloging-in-Publication Data

Barker, Marilyn Conover, 1932–
The Legacy of Mormon Furniture : the Mormon material culture,
undergirded by faith, commitment, and craftsmanship / written by
Marilyn Conover Barker ; photography by Scott Peterson.
p. cm.
Includes bibliographical references and index.
ISBN 0-87905-632-0
1. Furniture making. 2. Furniture, Mormon. I. Peterson, Scott
1951– . II. Title
TT194.B37 1995
749.213'08'8263—dc20   95-11533
                                          CIP

CONTENTS

Acknowledgments

Desmond J. Barker Jr., my husband, gave love, time, effort, and vast support.

Dr. Thomas Carter, professor, University of Utah, shared the results of many years of research in Utah material culture.

Gene Kunz, my friend, donated countless hours in historical archives verifying data.

Individuals from The Church of Jesus Christ of Latter-day Saints assisted in my research through church archives, as did others from the Museum of Church History and Art.

Dale Beecher, registrar, shared important records and data on each piece of furniture selected from the LDS Church collection for inclusion in this work.

Ronald Reed, Curator of Photography, located and loaned the historic photographs selected for the book from the LDS Church collection.

LDS Church museums and historical sites officials contributed information and permission to photograph their collections:

Beehive House, *Curator and Director:*	Margaret Adams
Cove Fort, *Director:*	Elder Carvel Jackson
Jacob Hamblin House, *Director:*	Elder Dixie Leavitt

Utah State Parks and Recreation Division representatives contributed information and permission to photograph their collections:

Division representative:	Karen Creeger
Pioneer Trail State Park, *Curator:*	William Ormond

Division of Utah State History officials contributed data, diaries, and photographs from their collection:

Curator of Photographs:	Susan Whetstone
Curator of Education:	Wreatha Witte
Coordinator of Collections:	Linda Thatcher

Howard Freed, Curator of Pioneer Village, Lagoon Corporation, permitted me to photograph their Mormon furniture collection.

Jeff Johnson, Director of Utah State Archives and Records Service contributed important documents and diaries for my research.

Anne Florence Hatch, Assistant Curator of Folk Arts for the Utah Arts Council contributed archival documentation.

Curators and representatives of the Daughters of the Utah Pioneers (DUP) organization were invaluable in their support for this book's authenticity, breadth, and depth. Museum and relic hall archivists invited me to document and photograph their collections, for which I am most appreciative:

Salt Lake City Museum, *Curator of Education:*	Edith Menna
Richmond, Cache County Relic Hall,	
Curator:	Isabelle Bright
Logan, Cache County Museum, *Curator:*	Virginia Parker
Parawan, Iron County, Rock Church Museum,	
Curator:	Barbara Burt
Nephi, Juab County Museum, *Curator:*	Elora Nebeker
St. George Museum, Washington County,	
Curator:	Delores Riggs
Representative:	Vera Dean Blackburn
Ogden Museum, Weber County, *Curator:*	Ruth White
Ephraim, Sanpete County Museum, *Curator:*	Virginia Nielsen

Mount Pleasant Relic Hall, Sanpete County,
    Curator: Ester Christensen
Orderville, Kane County Relic Hall,
    Curator: Clella Hepworth
Pleasant Grove Museum, Utah County,
    Curator: May Metta Johnson
American Fork Museum, Utah County,
    Curator: Wanda Snow Peterson

City Museums contributed information and access to their collections for photography:

Brigham City Museum and Gallery,
    Box Elder County, *Curators:*   Larry Douglas
                                        Kathy Bradford
Fairview, Sanpete County Museum *Curator:*   Ronald Staker
Fillmore State House Museum,
    Millard County, *Curator:*   Gordon J. Chatland
Richfield, Ralph Ramsay Home,
    Commissioner: Lois Christensen

    Stephen Shepherd, woodcrafting expert, prepared chapter five's material on painting and graining, and provided pioneer wood selection and construction information.

    Dale Peel shared his knowledge of Mormon furniture construction and Sanpete County private collections.

    John Told shared his knowledge of Mormon pioneer life and Scandinavian furniture. He also permitted photography of his personal furniture collection for this book.

    Todd Schvaneveldt shared his knowledge as a member of the photography team.

    Franklin K. Brough shared the diaries and life histories of Jacob G. Bigler and Bathsheba Bigler Smith.

    Elizabeth Conover Reynolds shared the diaries and life history of Peter Wilson Cownover.

    Decandants of cabinetmakers and chair makers shared diaries, life histories, and documented pieces of furniture.

Barbara B. Nielson on maker:	William L. N. Allen
Ted Bird on maker:	Edmund Fuller Bird
Rodney H. Brady on carpenter:	Lindsay Anderson Brady
Beverly B. Hansen on makers:	David and W. W. Cluff
Annie M. Jennings on maker:	Thomas Cottam
Donna C. Peterson on maker:	Mathew Dalton
Anna Lou Dinwoodey Jenkins on maker:	Henry Dinwoodey
Doris Reeder & Sharon Meikle on maker:	Dr. James Hancey
Gus Clark on maker:	Isaac Losser
Mrs. L. R. Nilsson on maker:	Hans Olson Magleby
Elizabeth C. Reynolds on maker:	Seeley Owen
Geraldene Ramsay Randall on maker:	Ralph Ramsay
Frank Swensen on maker:	Anders Swensen

    Antique dealers specializing in the procurement and sale of Utah furniture shared their unique information:

Jonathan Sweet of Honest Jon's Hill House Antiques in Salt Lake City
Lynn Carter of Carter's Antiques in Payson, Utah County
Gary Thompson of the Brass Key in Salt Lake City

THE POWER TO ESTABLISH STYLE

The Mormon pioneers emigrated to the Intermountain West from many states in the Union and countries of the world. What they first called Deseret became the territory of Utah, where they practiced their religion and established a unique culture. They lived in an era burgeoning with significant social, economic, and cultural diversity that was very different from our lifestyle today. The changing world affected their daily life as much as their changing landscape as they moved from place to place. What they brought with them and improvised along the way left a material legacy that is remarkable, considering the circumstances of the Mormons as individuals and as a colonizing group.

The Industrial Revolution, begun in England, created some of the Victorian attitudes and cultural tastes that moved to America. These attitudes of the time affected Mormon converts, influencing many of their decisions outside of religious beliefs.

Material culture documentation has been lacking to tell what life was like in 1847, when the first immigrant members of The Church of Jesus Christ of Latter-day Saints (the Mormons) arrived in the Utah Territory or when statehood was achieved in 1896. This book's contribution is intended to promote understanding of the importance of this legacy of influence on present-day Mormon culture and American material culture as a whole. Fortunately, journal-keeping has always been stressed in Mormon culture, and the journals, autobiographies, and other documents left by the immigrants and descendants of the 1800s have proven invaluable in understanding Mormon cultural dynamics, including the resultant material culture—most notably, their furniture.

As spiritual and colonizing leader of the Mormon Church, Brigham Young, himself a fine cabinetmaker, directed a furniture manufactory in Great Salt Lake City and gave encouragement and opportunity to many furniture craftsmen who came as converts from various countries.

Mormons often refer to Deseret and to Zion, and clarification of these terms here will be helpful to non-Mormons. *Deseret* is a Book of Mormon name for *honeybee*. Deseret as a geographical territory reflected the industry of its Mormon inhabitants likened to honeybees—busy, cooperative, and productive. Deseret appears as part of the name of several Utah businesses even today, and the beehive and the word *industry* are part of the great seal of the state of Utah. The beehive and the honeybee are symbols carved for Brigham Young by cabinetmaker and wood-carver Ralph Ramsay, as pictured on the jacket of this book. Other artisans in wood also embellished their work with the symbols of industry and cooperative endeavor for the good of the colony.

Zion is the spiritual gathering place for people committed to the work of the Lord in preparation for Christ's Second Coming. To many present-day Mormons, Zion is a spiritual state of mind while Deseret is a place.

Very little has been written of the material culture that gave voice to the everyday experience of living and creating a spiritual lifestyle in the American West. This book seeks to make a contribution toward filling that void, while introducing readers to the historical and contemporary craftsmen who are creating fresh interpretations of the classic furniture design legacy of early Mormon furniture makers. Mormon furniture collectors, interior designers, inheritors, and daily users of these pieces appreciate how comfortably this furniture may be incorporated into today's home and office decorating schemes.

Mormon pioneers were committed to the establishment of a refined society in a difficult desert environment, and no undertaking exemplifies that goal more clearly than the silk industry that drew on the knowledge and teaching of Susanne Gaudin Cardon. A convert from the Piedmont area of Italy, where she had cultivated silkworms and spun and woven silk, she and a wife of Brigham Young, Zina Young, demonstrated the art and encouraged women all over Utah to take up the industry. Harvesting silk cocoons, spinning, weaving, and sewing beautiful silk clothing was taken on with good spirit.

Silk clothing and decorative items to enhance the home were created in most Utah towns by and for the women who desired finer clothing and textiles than the frontier lifestyle provided. The industry of silk production also required growing mulberry trees to sustain the silk worms, definitely a long-term commitment.

The merging of furniture making with the production of silk throughout Utah, and cotton in southern Utah, for draperies, upholstery, and clothing created a lifestyle levels above the frontier life of western lore. The text and illustrations of this book should dispel any mystery some may have about Mormon values concerning the pursuit of excellence in craftsmanship, commerce, and lifestyle, as well as in personal and spiritual dealings with one another and those outside the church. The documentation of artifacts from Mormon pioneers communicates their ideas and values, bridging the culture of the past with the present. Since history is not the past but rather what people think of the past, so the documentation of an artifact that remains from the past opens ways in which ideas and values are communicated. We have learned a great deal about the pioneer Mormons by studying their furniture as artifacts that communicate the lifestyle of their time.

Furniture is a necessity and a most personal tool. Individual pieces document concepts of life in various eras with clues to personal experiences and expectations of life. To be appreciated objectively, an object made for a specific function or reason must be analyzed first according to its original artisan, tools and materials; then as it met its maker's or owner's expectations; and then its purchaser's. Finally, it may be appraised for its economic value.

Kenneth L. Ames, a historian of material culture, expresses the current approach to understanding history when he states:

> *Only illustrative material becomes the very stuff of history itself because the objects with which they once surrounded themselves take on increased importance as clues to their lives. A good deal of life is composed of unverbalized, subconscious, or quasi-conscious experiences of a variety of objects and environments in the world around us.*[1]

The objects Mormons used, whether made by a master cabinetmaker or by a handy neighbor, express the social dynamics of the time and place where they were created. The example for excellence in craftsmanship and high-style taste was established in the homes of church leaders and emulated by church members.

Brigham Young had a vision of creating an ideal society and an extensive empire called Deseret, which included not only Utah, but parts of Idaho, Nevada, Arizona, and California. His direction to the people to document their lives by word and artifact extended to all the towns the Mormons created in all of these states. Mormonism affected material culture throughout the Intermountain West.

To the Mormon immigrants, nothing was so highly prized as wood, next to the value of water and food. Wood was a necessity for shelter, furnishings, transportation, and fuel. The same limited supply was needed for all stages of establishing the culture in an arid, inhospitable, but beautiful environment. Mormon cabinetmakers were involved in all the stages of settlement. The woods available in the environs were not the hardwoods of their choice; but their technical skill and sense of style in painting and graining softwoods to look like hardwoods enabled them to create the elegance they and their public desired. The adaptations of designs from hardwood furniture to their innovative reinterpretations in softwood furniture created a style that can be identified as Mormon furniture.

Brigham Young's trade before becoming the Mormon leader was that of a cabinetmaker and carpenter. It was natural for him to document the colonization of Zion by having furniture made from the hardwood wagon boxes that he used to carry his belongings across the plains. Subsequent supplies and equipment ordered from eastern cities designated the woods that were to be used for emigrants' shipping containers. The crates were disassembled and used to make furniture in the new settlements.

Most Mormon craftsmen were literate and felt compelled to write journals and diaries. The contribution of these furniture makers to the colonization effort was appreciated by their contemporaries, who also recorded information about them in documents of their own. We have been able to document a surprising number of these fine tradesmen through credible sourcing of their work.

Converts came largely from Great Britain and Scandinavia. Most initial members of the church came from British backgrounds and had lived in New York, Vermont, Massachusetts, Virginia, Mississippi, Pennsylvania, and Ohio prior to moving to Missouri and Illinois, and then emigrating to the West.

Social and economic backgrounds varied widely. Mormons suffered persecutions and lost family members and resources of all types, including farms, businesses, personal property, and cash. By the time the Mormons entered the valley of the Great Salt Lake, their resources were largely limited to their faith, their tools, and their desire to establish a new society on the edge of a barren desert.

The use of church-backed scrip, barter, cooperation, and a great deal of determined ingenuity, combined with a religious belief that established a social and spiritual organization, caused these people to work for the common good with the goal of creating an ideal civilization.

Many of the cabinetmakers who immigrated to Utah were supported financially by the church for their trip; in order to pay back their debt, they did work for the church after their arrival. They found work in the entire territory throughout the nineteenth century. The number of craftsmen fluctuated region by region according to development. As eastern factories began to deliver furniture by rail, the craftsmen tended to move to areas not yet served by the railroad. The regional workshops continued throughout the last third of the nineteenth century, but fewer and fewer cabinetmakers could sustain themselves by their craft alone. They added other skills and products to their service. Those with retailing or carpentry skills prospered.

Many cabinetmakers and chair makers became both church and community leaders. The histories of local events in Mormon communities included these men and their families. Family pride in the ancestor who was a cabinetmaker impelled many people to participate in this book. In addition, the willingness of key individuals to share information, diaries, and furniture collections held by the Mormons and the church enabled Scott Peterson to photograph furniture and aided my efforts to compile this important history.

The legacy left by the builders and wood-carvers of pioneer days in Utah can be appreciated not only in Mormon Church archives today, but in the many museums and other public and private collections of original and reproduction high-style—and simple—Mormon furniture.

It is my intent to introduce readers to the hard-won and grand legacy of furnishings that should be appreciated for their beauty and innovation. This book gives insight into the lives and values of a most unique people.

Marilyn Conover Barker

NOTES

1. Ames, Kenneth L., "Victorian Furniture," essays from a Victorian Society Autumn Symposium, *Victorian Society in America* 8, nos. 3, 4 (1982): 10–14.

2. Figure numbers for illustrations throughout the book begin with the chapter designation; i.e: chapter one, illustration sixteen (figure 1.16).

EUROPEAN ORIGINS OF THE FURNITURE LEGACY

✳   ✳   ✳

THE COURAGE TO CREATE ZION PLANTED HIGH STYLE IN THE UTAH WILDERNESS

Learning from the material culture of a people opens a dialogue with the past and creates an understanding documented by the objects they used in their daily lives. This behavioral approach to historical analysis includes the experience of the objects' owners as well as the individual makers and their roles as members of a group. The remnants of familiar items, such as chairs, tools, dishes, and houses, provide a clearer understanding of the time and lifestyle of any people being studied. Appreciating the determination of the Mormon pioneers to establish an educated, genteel, and cooperative society based on, and lived according to, Christian teachings and practices is manifested eloquently through their cherished belongings.

This material-culture dialogue with the Mormon past encompasses not only the Utah territory they called Deseret, but also many of the states of New England, the Midwest, the Rocky Mountain area, the Southwest, and Southern California. In these many locations, a religiously focused people established farms, towns, and cities. The resulting civilization continues to speak to all people throughout the world.

The material evidence of the Mormon pioneers, today preserved in museums and private collections, serves as a genealogical and historical treasure trove for those seeking to appreciate this religious group's contribution to the formative years of America. Forced to move, adjust, colonize, build, and rebuild their homes, this people's furniture illuminates the story of early Mormon life made more poignant by quotes from their diaries.

Members of The Church of Jesus Christ of Latter-day Saints, known throughout the world as Mormons, believed in God and his Son Jesus

FIGURE 1.1

FAMILY, WAGON TRAIN
Collection of Utah State Historical Society

Christ, as did many God-fearing frontier people. What made the Mormons different was their unique Christian belief that revelation continues to occur on earth and is constantly changing and expanding with the people and the times. These revelations were given to their prophet, designated by God to receive divine revelation. In addition to the Holy Bible, they accept as scripture the Book of Mormon; the Doctrine and Covenants, which are a compilation of major revelations and instructions given through the church's founder, Joseph Smith, and a few additions since his time; and the Pearl of Great Price, containing certain translations and writings of Joseph Smith.

The first prophet and the Mormon Church's founder, Joseph Smith lived from 1805 until his death at the hands of a mob in 1844. The second prophet and president, who moved the people to Utah after the murder of Joseph Smith, was Brigham Young. He lived from 1801 until 1877. It was during his time that most of the furniture discussed in this book was created, and Young had a profound influence on the material culture that developed among the Mormons because of his own background as a carpenter, joiner, glazier, and furniture maker.

From the time young Joseph Smith told his Protestant minister that he had experienced a spiritual revelation, he, his family, their friends, and their followers were persecuted. Subjected to mob fury in Kirtland, Ohio, and in several places in Missouri, the Latter-day Saints received no state protection against life-threatening harassment. Moving again in 1839, they found a new place on the banks of the Mississippi River in Illinois. They named it Nauvoo, and by 1844 it rivaled St. Louis, Missouri, as the most important city of the the upper Mississippi Valley. This city evolved from a temporary town of log cabins and tents to a permanent city with two-story brick homes, wide streets, and stylish buildings that housed the needs of administration and religious worship. The multistoried Nauvoo Temple could be seen for miles up and down the river and was a significant landmark for the entire Mississippi culture.

Work was plentiful for carpenters and cabinetmakers not only in Nauvoo, but in surrounding towns and cities such as St. Louis and Chicago. Mormon craftsmen worked then and later in individual shops or in larger cooperative factories. The workshops and the methods and knowledge of manufacture were subject to the traditions brought from their former homes throughout America and Europe, especially Great Britain and Scandinavia.

Mormons living on the Mississippi River included every new convert—regardless of social, ethnic, regional, or international background. The Nauvoo Covenant assured emigrants: "We take all the Saints with us to the extent of our ability, that is our influence and property." Even those of least financial means were welcomed, but the cooperative endeavor included people from all economic levels.

TECHNICAL INVENTIONS INFLUENCED FURNITURE STYLE TRENDS

With the introduction of a circular veneer saw to early-nineteenth-century America, cabinetmakers could slice veneers much thinner than with hand-saws. Exotic woods such as rosewood became more widely used, and the *American Empire style* developed. The introduction of steam-driven lathes between 1820 and 1840 contributed to the popularity of turned Roman legs on American Empire furniture. Turned legs in Utah were used on a variety of furniture styles. These same lathes easily made turned *"spooled furniture,"* which became so popular that the style was named after the famous Swedish opera star Jenny Lind. Spool-turned decoration became an important style characteristic throughout America, and it was modeled in Nauvoo and later in Utah. The spool-turned elements were first sliced in half, then painted and glued or nailed to the pieces of furniture.[1] (figure 1.2)

By 1844, an estimated twenty-five thousand Mormons resided in Nauvoo and nearby villages. The economic policy of the community emphasized the importance of manufacturing and the necessity of local production. Nauvoo had steam-powered sawmills, a steam-powered flour mill, a tool factory, a foundry, and a factory for china-ware. The newest styles were sought and incorporated into existing designs, with stress placed on fine quality.

The most fashionable style of furniture in early-nineteenth-century America was imported from France. *French Empire furniture*, named in honor of the expanding empire of Napoleon, had graceful S curves that harked back to Greek and Roman antiquities. Understandably, the English who adopted it renamed it *Regency*. English cabinetmakers were making their own adaptations of ancient Greek furniture depicted on Greek vases. They shipped their Regency furniture to America via New York. Americans called the style *American Empire*. Furniture makers in New York City and New York State considered the enthusiasm for variations on the Empire style very fortuitous. Their southern markets, especially around the lower

FIGURE 1.2

CRADLE

Anonymous maker
Hardwood, walnut stained, spool turned
38 x 22 x 36 in.
Belonged to Emma and Joseph Smith
Collection of The Church of Jesus Christ
of Latter-day Saints (LDS)

FIGURE 1.3

EMPIRE BED
Anonymous maker
Pine, painted and grained, faux mahogany
43 x 48 x 68 in.

ROD-BACK CHAIR
Walter Huish
Pine
30 x 16 in.
Seat height: 15 in.
Both, Collection of John Told

Mississippi River, were receptive to the graceful Empire lines that enhanced their elegant new towns and opulent plantation homes. America had long identified with the ancient ideals of Greek and Roman civilizations. The fashionable motifs applied to eighteenth-century furniture were variations of Greek and Roman motifs, such as acanthus leaves, shells, and architectural pediments. The Empire period's classical designs were used with greater attention to historical accuracy. Understanding the furniture styles of preference in Nauvoo is important because they were the first styles undertaken in the softwoods of Utah, where adaptations were immediately necessary.

The *Empire gondola chair* that was popular in the Mississippi culture became one of the early designs made in settling Utah. The Mississippi (late Empire) gondola form had a lyre-shaped splat and a plain, uncarved surface. Even though the wood used in Utah changed the proportions of this chair, the lyre or the fiddle-shaped splat was common. Beds and other pieces of furniture had many of these same elements. (figures 1.3, 1.4, 1.5)

The Mormon people of Nauvoo were convinced that the United States

was a unique place with a special mission. Many of the democratic principles of the ancient Greeks were consistent with American ideals.

Because the nineteenth century was a period of rapid, complex, and widespread socio-economic upheaval, the influence of England and continental Europe on American taste is undeniable. Any explanation of nineteenth-century taste must include the forces of modernization and tradition—often in conflict with one another. This conflict was apparent in the furniture styles produced in Nauvoo, because both European taste and contemporary crafts techniques that were possible with the newest mechanical inventions were evident there.

FIGURE 1.4

EMPIRE GONDOLA CHAIR
Public Works, G.S.L.C., 1856
Pine, painted and grained, faux mahogany
35 x 15 in.
Collection of LDS Church, at Lagoon
 Corporation

FIGURE 1.5

CHESS GAME TABLE & CHAIR
Parley P. Pratt, made 1860
Probably hickory and maple
Made from hardwood packing boxes
 in first wagon train, 1847
Table: 30 x 24 (diameter) in.
Chair: 34 x 18 in.
Seat height: 16 in.
Collection of Salt Lake City Daughters
 25of the Utah Pioneers (DUP)

UNITY WITHIN THE GROWING MORMON MOVEMENT THREATENED NON-MORMONS, CAUSING THE FORMATION OF THE NAUVOO LEGION

Because Mormon populations grew so rapidly in new areas where they settled, they displaced many other groups of differing religious beliefs. Those very dynamics united them, and their formidable voting power was seen as a threat by their non-Mormon neighbors. Nauvoo was on the frontier, where politics were rough. Having been harassed in the East, they felt the need to protect themselves from robbery, arson, rape, and murder, which had forced them to leave previously established communities.

The Nauvoo Mormons formed an independent city militia for their protection. This three-to-four-thousand-member volunteer group, called the Nauvoo Legion, protected the townspeople from troublemakers as best they could. However, the harassment continued, and the seeds of trouble recognized as early as 1842 forced them to plan for an eventual move to the West.[2]

CIVIL UNREST IN NAUVOO LED TO PLANS TO MOVE WEST

The unrest in the Nauvoo area worsened, and Joseph Smith prophesied in August of 1842 that "the Saints would continue to suffer much affliction and would be driven to the Rocky Mountains . . . some of you will live to go and assist in making settlements and build cities and see the Saints become a mighty people in the midst of the Rocky Mountains."[3]

Recognizing his personal danger, Prophet Joseph Smith told the Nauvoo Legion not to try to protect him. He didn't want bloodshed nor the loss of any more Saints through murder. Smith was imprisoned in the Carthage jail, then murdered by a masked mob on 27 June 1844. The Nauvoo settlers realized they would have to leave their homes, temple, and the town they had built.[4]

A Mormon temple is a special building where sacred ordinances are performed, such as marriages. Many of the finest carpenters and cabinetmakers worked on the Nauvoo Temple, and later on the temples built in pioneer Utah. The workmanship of these carefully chosen artisans was considered the best by the people of those times.

By the fall of 1845, the Mormons announced that they would leave Nauvoo and move west the following spring. In the October conference held in the new temple, Apostle Parley P. Pratt observed, "The Lord designs to lead us to a wider field of action, where there will be no one to say we crowd them, and where we can enjoy the pure principles of liberty and equal rights."[5]

During the winter of 1845–46, Nauvoo became a supply center for thousands of wagons being readied for the exodus. Bathsheba Bigler Smith, wife of Apostle George A. Smith and cousin of Joseph Smith, wrote that the city was one vast workshop, "nearly every family was wagon building. Our parlor became a shop in which to paint wagons and likewise, every other parlor in the neighborhood was put to some such use in the general preparation for the exodus."[6]

Peter Wilson Cownover's* journal reported the urgency of the moving preparations:

* The Cownover name changed from its original Dutch-emigrant spelling in 1625—Van Kowenhoven—to Covenhoven seven generations later when family members fought in the Revolutionary War, to Cownover in 1800s, and finally the family changed it to Conover in 1888.

> The mob began to burn out the Saints at Green Plains, twenty-five miles below Nauvoo. I was called on to raise a company of ninety wagons, with two men to each wagon, and we started down. It was a fearful time. Women and children were wading around in mud and snow, wet through and no place to go. I continued helping to move them until the sheriff called a posse to go and make them stop the burning. We went down and found the mob burning a house and dancing a war dance. They did dance, but it was upon their horses. We chased them about six miles, but most of them got away into the state of Missouri. After that I went to hauling for the burned-out brethren.[7]

The planned spring departure was moved up by such mob violence that making a February escape in the middle of a fierce winter was imperative for many. Six hundred people crossed the ice-covered Mississippi River to safety. Others went after the spring thaw.

Bathsheba Bigler Smith's autobiography told of leaving her Nauvoo home:

> We left a comfortable home, the accumulation of four years of labor and thrift, and took away with us only a few much-needed articles such as clothing, bedding, and provisions. We left everything else behind us for our enemies. My last act in that precious spot was to tidy the rooms, sweep up the floor, and set the broom in its accustomed place behind the door.[8]

Though well organized, the fleeing Mormons were overwhelmed by cold, mud, and hunger. Cholera and malaria added to their miseries by the time they moved into Sugar Creek, Iowa, and on to camps established at intervals along the route west. The main town settlements were Kanesville, now known as Council Bluffs, on the eastern bank of the Missouri River; and Winter Quarters, now known as Florence, Nebraska, on the Missouri's western bank. The loss of life was great in the harsh weather and wilderness. Many families had been forced to leave their furnishings behind or to barter them for supplies.

Unfortunately, the Nauvoo Temple was burned by mobs after the Mormons left to go west. Little of the building's structure remains, and the only piece of furniture retrieved from the fire was a spooled and painted, three-seated pine assembly chair.[9] (figure 1.6)

Cownover's wife Eveline died in Winter Quarters, Nebraska. This journal account is but an example of thousands of Mormons who experienced similar hardships:

> There I was left with ten children, the youngest but two years of age. Brothers Brigham and Heber Kimball came to see how I was faring. They told me that they had a widow lady for me to take to the Valley to take care of my family. I did not like the idea but they insisted as they knew I needed someone to take care of the children. Her name was Percilla Pearson. She and Jane McCarl made the clothes my children wore when crossing the Plains.

Cownover was not interested in arranged marriages or polygamy. He was among the majority of Mormon men who felt that way.[10]

Mormon families were generally large, and an estimated one-third were polygamous. Most polygamous marriages were two-wife families. Many Mormon homes provided help for the poor and unfortunate either as helpers or as wives. Large polygamous families required specialization. The pattern of settlement was affected by these family units attempting to be as self-sufficient as possible. They were also part of the society as a whole that subsisted on the barter system.

Brigham Young's great organizing ability and practical, spiritual leadership set a powerful example of enthusiasm for those who wondered about their destinies when the harsh realities of survival became acute. Early Mormons drew strength from Young's belief that all would be as promised.

Attitude was a key to survival. William Clayton, the secretary to

Brigham Young and a scribe of the pioneer experience, had to leave his wife Diantha in Nauvoo. She was expecting a child and was unable to make the trying journey in February. Many stayed in Nauvoo at extreme risk. Clayton wrote in his journal on 15 April 1846, when word finally reached him of the birth of their son, "Truly I feel to rejoice at this intelligence, but feel sorry to hear of her [Diantha's] sickness. This morning I composed a new song—All is Well."[11]

The words Clayton wrote to an existing hymn became the song of courage for all the emigrants. Known today as "Come, Come, Ye Saints," it has appeared in every Mormon hymnbook since 1851. It reflects an attitude and toughness that manifested itself throughout the entire Mormon culture.

Come, come, ye Saints, no toil nor labor fear; But with joy wend your way.
Though hard to you this journey may appear, Grace shall be as your day.
'Tis better far for us to strive Our useless cares from us to drive;
Do this, and joy your hearts will swell—All is well! All is well!

Why should we mourn or think our lot is hard? 'Tis not so; all is right.
Why should we think to earn a great reward If we now shun the fight?
Gird up your loins; fresh courage take. Our God will never us forsake;
And soon we'll have this tale to tell—All is well! All is well!

Singing, dancing, and theatricals became an important part of Mormon life. Pioneers worked to make life rich with cultural offerings. The priority given to music, drama, and education was significant.

ECONOMIC AND PHYSICAL CHALLENGES PRESSED MORMONS TO GREATER COLONIZATION EFFORTS

Economic survival was always a basic challenge in the colonization story of Mormon emigrants. The Latter-day Saints as a religious body, being well organized and focused cooperatively on their goals, came to play a unique role in American history.

In an arrangement among President James K. Polk; his Secretary of War, William L. Marcy; and Mormon representative Jesse C. Little, a carriage- and cabinetmaker, it was agreed that the U.S. Army would recruit five hundred young Mormon men. This Mormon Battalion was ordered to march from Winter Quarters, Nebraska, to Santa Fe, New Mexico, with a destination in California. The military service was valued in the thousands of dollars, a great deal of money in those days. But the absence of these men on the wagon trains going west made it necessary for women, old men, and youngsters to drive the ox teams.

FIGURE 1.7

LADDER-BACK ROCKER
William Clayton
Brought from Nauvoo by Clayton's
  wife Diantha
Hardwood, painted and stenciled,
  leather seat
32 x 21 in.
Seat height: 14 in.
Collection of Ogden DUP

The money was used to buy supplies for the poorer emigrants and for the erection of a gristmill to supply flour to all, both of which helped offset the loss of the strongest young men of the church. Many of the soldiers became involved in the first California gold rush when they reached their destination, contributing even more financial support to the Mormon economy. Soldiers returning from the gold fields brought goods, including furniture, which had been shipped by boat to California.

The 143 men, 3 wives, and 2 children who comprised the first group of Saints selected to explore and make way for the subsequent expeditions to the valley of the Great Salt Lake were predominantly New England Americans. There were Canadians, English, Irish, Bavarians, Danes, and Scots in lesser numbers.

Those selected to be the original settlers were chosen for their ability to make roads, to build bridges, to erect temporary quarters, and to provide food by hunting. Among them were mechanics, carpenters, wheelwrights, masons, and cabinetmakers. Those first settlers were a strong and practical group who gathered together in the Salt Lake Valley on 24 July 1847. Some in scouting parties had arrived ahead of the main party, but the date of July 24th is marked as their official arrival.[12]

FIGURE 1.8

SMALL, FIDDLEBACK ROCKER
Anonymous maker
Primitive unmilled wood, painted and
    grained, faux mahogany
42 x 17½ in.
Seat height: 12 in.
Collection of LDS Church

HARDWOOD PACKING BOXES AND WAGON PARTS WERE OF HIGH-STYLE IMPORTANCE

All supplies of the first exploration group and those of all the subsequent wagon trains were organized for the trip in hardwood boxes that could withstand dramatic changes in temperature and moisture and months of jolting on the trail.

The desert destination of the Mormon pioneers was, at best, sparsely wooded, and the valley was virtually treeless. The need for wood made the packing boxes even more valuable. The settlers lived for a while in their wagons and also used their boxes as tables, chairs, chests, and cupboards. All had needs for some furniture before knowledge of the woods of the unexplored areas was developed and lumber mills were built. Naturally, boxes made of preferred hardwoods were precious to the pioneers. Master cabinetmakers were hired to create lovely pieces of furniture. Items made from these boxes

FIGURE 1.9

MISSIONARY BOX
Anonymous maker
Wagon-box parts, grained and stamped
19 x 33 x 20 in.
Shipped to Missouri, returned to Moroni
Collection of David & Roselle Hamblin

FIGURE 1.10

BENCH
Anonymous maker
Made from packing box, partitions left
  to keep bench stable
26 x 57 x 12 in.
Collection of Ann Carter

ranged from benches, where the box pieces could still be identified, to very
fine inlaid tables that used a variety of woods from many boxes. The packing boxes were an available resource of milled-wood varieties about which
craftsmen were knowledgeable. They created a variety of styles according to
their skills and the design preference of the client. Many pieces of family
furniture were made from the boxes as a way of documenting the pioneer
trek. (figures 1.5, 1.8, 1.9, 1.10)

CULTURALLY DIVERSE CRAFTSMEN CREATED ECLECTIC
FURNITURE STYLES

Though materials dictated some direction of the designs, the knowledgeable
and diverse cabinetmakers were supremely innovative within the constraints
of their limited material resources. Once settled in the western wilderness,
Scandinavian, English, Irish, European, and New England cabinetmakers,
each resolved wood-type material challenges and design execution in his
own unique way.

By 1855, English cabinetmakers emigrating straight from London were
producing styles fashionable in their homeland. William Bell was a master
craftsman whose London shop had produced high-style English designs for
twenty years. He built furniture in the newest *Victorian Gothic style* for his •

FIGURE 1.11

CHAIR
Rufus C. Allen
Pine, rawhide seat and back
37 x 20 in.
Seat height: 17 in.
Used in original fort at Santa Clara
Collection at Jacob Hamblin Home,
  LDS Church

Utah patron, church president Brigham Young, before the American eastern seaboard cabinetmakers had even imported the designs to their own shops, which were the fashion trendsetters for the young nation.

Mormon cabinetmakers were encouraged by their leaders to exercise creative freedom and individual ideas about beauty and function. Leadership welcomed diversity and adaptation of the many styles that were emerging with the new technologies. At no time did the Mormon Church sponsor design style that could represent their religious philosophy. Mormons were encouraged to sponsor excellent craftsmanship, but design was left to the choice of the individual cabinetmaker and buyer. The most fashionable styles were the most popular, and cabinetmakers tried to include their personal adaptations of those styles.

The challenge of supplying the necessary items for settlement was acute. The need for shelter and furniture was ranked with the need for food. Immediately upon arrival, the trees of the area were examined for their usefulness. Ten days after the arrival of the first pioneers into the valley of the

FIGURE 1.12

RECTILINEAR STYLE CHAIR
Anonymous maker
Pine
44 x 18 in.
Seat height: 16 in.
Combined ladder-back and rod-back
    elements, with turned stretcher wings
    for resting
Belonged to Brigham Young
Collection of Pioneer Trail State Park

Great Salt Lake, Howard Egan wrote in his journal: "We cut down and brought to camp two cedars for the purpose of making bedsteads and pails Etc." That same first company also planted five acres of potatoes, which they hoped would provide seed potatoes for the next year.[13] (figure 1.11)

The time frame of the first furniture made from indigenous materials was determined by how quickly the sawmills could be erected, lathes set up, and roads built to access available woods. Since many cabinetmakers had never worked with the "inferior" softwoods, they needed to experiment and redesign structural parts—such as chair and table legs—to accommodate weight at angles cooperative with the grain of the wood available. The pine they found in abundance had far fewer large knots than the pine they considered inferior wood for furniture in the northeastern forests. But the grain wasn't as fine as some of the hardwood trees they admired and were used to working with in furniture making. As they became more secure with wilderness woods, and some of the finer crafting tools arrived or were made, they produced finer wood furniture out of the red and yellow pine, cottonwood, box elder, and black willow found in Utah.

Rectilinear design based on the square was pleasing to the practical, organized sensibilities of the Mormon town planners and homebuilders, and it was carried over into the earliest furniture. However, because Empire-style furniture was especially desired by all Mormons, whether from America, England, or Europe, it became the design favored by the emerging middle class. It was produced quickly after the first emigrants arrived. The fine wood veneers that had been affixed to urban pieces of furniture were impossible to re-create in the softwoods of the wilderness. But the high art of covering pine with a painted and grained surface to resemble the finer woods was very acceptable. (figure 1.12, 1.13)

FIGURE 1.13

BLANKET CHEST
Anonymous maker
Hardwood, primitive graining
29 x 20 x 36 in.
Collection of Richard Blanck

The isolation from design centers of major metropolitan areas was real, but communication with the rest of America and the world was never interrupted because the Mormon Trail became a two-way trail. Not only did it facilitate all shipping and emigrant travel to Utah and beyond, but missionaries and goods returned by wagon trains to the eastern United States. The trail accommodated heavy travel until the railroad linked the Utah Territory to the East and West Coasts much later in 1869.

Shortly after the first Mormon pioneers' arrival, part of the original pioneer company formed a small group on 17 August 1847, which included Brigham Young and cabinetmaker-wheelwright Seeley Owen, to return on the trail to intercept the second wagon train headed for the valley of the Great Salt Lake. They met the wagon train, gave directions and information, and then returned to Winter Quarters, Iowa, to prepare the larger migration group scheduled to leave the following spring. This return trip, covering a rugged-terrain distance of 1,032 miles, was accomplished in nine weeks and three days.

Widower Seeley Owen returned to Utah with his only daughter in 1848 and established his business and home. Owen brought his tools and was able to set up a lathe, as his chair shows considerable skill compared to the earliest pieces produced in 1847. His daughter, Ann Owen Cownover, later recorded, "Father made all the furniture for our home." Those who had cabinetmaking skills made their first furniture, along with their homes, and then established themselves either as cabinetmakers or as carpenters to build the shelters and homes for others.[14] (figure 2.1)

The migration to the valley of the Great Salt Lake, counting the influx from California, Mississippi, and other groups, totaled 1,681 people who spent the winter of 1847–48 in the valley. This number swelled to approximately 20,000 by 1852, and in the next seventeen years—before the completion of the transcontinental railway—70,000 Saints had made the journey. It was no small accomplishment, for many of the people had become destitute through the forced sale of their homes and the trek over a thousand miles of wilderness plains and mountains. With their bare hands, the simplest tools, and creative grit, the pioneers built new homes in a barren land.

Mormons weren't the only ones on the trail, and people who met on the trail exchanged information. It is estimated that forty to fifty thousand

FIGURE 1.14

ROD-BACK CHAIR
Anonymous maker
Public Works, G.S.L.C.
Red pine, painted
31 x 18½ in.
Seat height: 15½ in.
Collection of Richard Blanck

prospectors journeyed overland to the California gold fields in 1849 and an equal number in 1850. These people were on the trail during the same months as the Mormons, and about fifteen-thousand people passed through the Salt Lake Valley each year. The people who were going to the gold fields became a significant economic help to the valley economy. Gold miners traded their heavy wagons, worn-out cattle, and merchandise for a horse or mule outfit to carry them quickly to their California destination. They were also not as organized as the Mormons, so when their wagons broke down or their equipment didn't work, they left it on the trail. The Mormon wagon trains picked up the discards, fixed them, and brought them to the Great Salt Lake Valley.[15] (figure 1.15)

SETTLEMENTS EVOLVED IN VARIOUS STAGES OF DEVELOPMENT WITHIN THE SAME TIME PERIOD

The communities to which individual craftsmen were assigned varied in their stages of development. Until peaceful agreements with the Indian tribes could be achieved, each community began with people living in their wagons, digging dugouts, and then building walls for small forts with houses attached to the walls. The Indians, whose lifestyle was at best disrupted and often destroyed by the new settlements, reacted to displacement in a variety of ways, including raids on property and on people. The policy of the church was to befriend and help the Indian people, but the new lifestyle and limited supplies caused breakdowns in negotiations, and sometimes, people on both sides were injured or killed.

FINANCIAL SUPPORT FOR CRAFTSMEN AND OTHER MORMON EMIGRANTS CAME FROM THE PERPETUAL EMIGRATION FUND OF THE CHURCH

The commitment of the church to bring the poor as well as those who could afford to outfit themselves, created an organization of competent agents who would help the migrations along. Assisting every person who wanted to emigrate to Utah necessitated the formation of the Perpetual Emigration Fund, administered by the church. This fund was supplied by all Mormons giving 10 percent of their increase (tithing) to the church.

A bishop and Perpetual Emigration Fund agent in Kanesville, Iowa, was

Jacob G. Bigler, a Virginia plantation owner who had sold the family property in Virginia and moved to Missouri about the time the mobs were burning homes and killing the Mormon people. The Bigler family, whose history included governors of Maryland, had a totally different lifestyle thrust upon them.

For three years, Bigler was the protector and organizer of the people awaiting emigration to the Utah Territory. Every person had food, clothing, household goods, tools, and furniture, which was either arranged in wagons or left for others. Great numbers of furniture pieces were left, and some were traded for supplies.

Each time the Biglers moved, they took less, but each time they moved, Jacob G. Bigler took the same small, practical chair to be used in the wagon. He never parted with that chair, and it became a symbolic reminder of his pioneer experience. In his old age, he had the chair's legs cut down so he could get closer to the ground to weed his raspberry patch.[16] (figure 1.16)

This traditional chair is indicative of many early American pieces that traveled to Utah and became icons of the pioneer experience. Such a chair was included in most wagons, but so was a surprising amount of porcelains. They were lovingly taken to Utah by a people who wanted the same level of comfort and culture they had left behind.

On his way to the gold fields in California, Mathew Dalton, an Irishman from Racine, Wisconsin, decided to stay the fall and winter of 1850 in the settlement of Ogden, Utah. His first job was to make furniture from the trees he hauled. He recorded in his journal: "The idea came to me that it would be wise to get me some good house logs; put up a shop to work in; and then start to make furniture for the people. Thus, I could find employment for myself during the winter months, as well as supply an urgent need of the people." He made a trip to Great Salt Lake City and purchased a lathe for wood turning. Next, he gathered his materials on the "Bottoms of the Weber River." He found and hauled such native trees as box elder, scrub oak, and cottonwood, and gathered green rushes to be used for "bottoming" his chairs.

He earned $430 in his shop that winter. After supplying his neighbors, he accumulated a surplus of furniture, procured a huge hayrack, and loaded it with chairs, tables, and bedsteads. He hauled them to Salt Lake City and called upon President Brigham Young, who commended him for his act and praised his work. Young purchased some furniture and introduced him to his counselor Heber C. Kimball, Apostle Jedediah Grant, and church historian Willard Richards. They all purchased Dalton's furniture, paying

FIGURE 1.16

CHAIR
Anonymous maker
Hardwood, leather seat
36 x 16 in.
Seat height: 15 in.
Chair belonged to Jacob G. Bigler
Collection of Nephi DUP

primarily in wheat. Later, Dalton joined the Mormon Church and established a furniture factory in Perry, Box Elder County.[17] (figure 1.17)

Economics played a major role in what belongings were brought and what method of transportation was used to take them to Utah. For example, one emigrant lined his wagon with tin, expecting to become a tinsmith in Utah. He was also a musician and included his piano in the wagon. When the trip became too difficult and the burden of the cherished piano too impractical, he dug a hole along the trail large enough to hold the piano, lined it with tin, covered it over with dirt, and proceeded to Utah. One year later, he traveled back to the site, unearthed his piano, and hauled it on to his new home.

The ingenuity and sacrifice required to bring musical instruments to Utah exemplifies the importance that the Mormons placed on music. The instruments themselves are as integral a part of Mormon material culture as the furniture. A notable characteristic of the Mormon cabinetmakers was the leadership they gave to the musical and theatrical entertainments of the settlements to which they were assigned.

Equipment, tools, templates, nails, and light machinery were brought along with household necessities. Each wagon driver was instructed to bring seeds of all kinds, and many brought tree saplings as well. Isaac Chase, a miller from Vermont, left Nauvoo with three wagons, one of which was loaded with milling equipment and driven by his thirteen-year-old daughter, Louisa. Chase's mill became one of the first lumber and flour mills in the valley of the Great Salt Lake. Such suppliers of valuable milled wood were critical to the success of cabinetmakers and carpenters.[18]

MISSIONARY WORK BROUGHT ENGLISH EMIGRANTS, INCLUDING MANY SKILLED CRAFTSMEN

By 1852, the church leaders turned their attention to the thirty thousand Latter-day Saints living in England. Many needed part or all of the financial assistance required to make the six-month trip from England to the Salt Lake Valley. Three kinds of companies were developed: 1) emigrants who paid ten pounds for emigration; costs exceeding that amount were subsidized; 2) emigrants who were totally subsidized; 3) emigrants who paid their own way but were organized and dispatched by the Perpetual Emigration

Fund. The amount of debt incurred determined the amount of time it would take indebted individuals to become financially independent in the new land. They were expected to contribute their time and skills to Public Works projects that assisted in establishing communities and enterprises such as a furniture factory for producing chairs. Skills were recognized and assignments were given for the betterment of the entire group. For those whose entire voyage and overland journey had been financed through the fund, working off their debt took several years.

Outstanding craftsmen were encouraged to emigrate to Utah. An epistle written in the Mormon Church newspaper, the *Millennial Star*, December 1847 stated:

> *To all Saints in England, Scotland, Ireland, Wales and the adjacent island and countries, we say emigrate as speedily as possible to this vicinity . . . bringing with you all kinds of choice seeds, of grain, vegetables, fruit shrubbery, trees and vines, everything that will please the eye, gladden the heart or cheer the soul of man that grows upon the face of the whole earth; also the best stock of beast, bird or fowl of every kind; also the best tools of every description and machinery for spinning, weaving, and dressing cotton, wool, flax and silk . . . so far as it can be consistently done, bring models and drafts and let the machinery be built when it is used, which will save great expense in transportation, particularly in heavy machinery and tools and implements generally.[19]*

From 1849 to 1855, some sixteen thousand European and English emigrants had been transported to Utah, including a large number of outstanding craftsmen who were able to contribute to the emerging culture.

A contemporary compilation of the skills of the English and European emigrants leaving Liverpool, England, during the period between 1850 and 1854 runs alphabetically from accountant to yeoman, and includes 96 boot and shoemakers, 10 boilermakers, 12 cabinetmakers, 46 engineers, 2 ironmongers, 226 miners, 73 masons, 8 printers, 22 spinners, 9 weavers, and some 300 other specialized-skill individuals.[20]

The emigration organization was carefully documented by the English author Charles Dickens in his book *The Uncommercial Traveler*. He referred to the eight hundred Mormon emigrants he watched departing England on the ship the *Amazon*, referring to them as "the pick and flower of England." Dickens added:

> *They had not been a couple of hours on board when they established their own police, made their own regulatives, and set their own watches at all the hatchways. Before nine o'clock the ship was orderly and as quiet as a man of war.*

There was no disorder, hurry or difficulty. I went over the Amazon's side feeling it impossible to deny that so far some remarkable influence had produced a remarkable result, which better known influences have often missed.[21]

English and Scandinavian cabinetmakers who came in the 1850s and 1860s were outstanding in their skill but were generally poor. By contrast, the American cabinetmaker had a higher social and economic lifestyle. Emigrating cabinetmakers from England, some at the master level of skill, had to accept indebting themselves to the Perpetual Emigration Fund to make the move. Master craftsmen such as Ralph Ramsay even assisted in building the handcarts his group used to cross the wilderness.

HANDCART TRANSPORTATION WAS DEVELOPED FOR REASONS OF ECONOMY AND SPEED

In 1855, Deseret suffered a famine due to cricket and grasshopper plagues that made it necessary to buy some food supplies. This catastrophe, coupled with the expense of maintaining the oxen and wagons during the slow trip west, stretched financial resources to the limit. In addition, deaths from cholera and malaria were mounting in the established outfitting communities of Nebraska and Iowa. The necessity of moving people out more rapidly became critical.

Brigham Young had long felt that people would be better off on the trail if they weren't encumbered with the slow, lumbering, ox-drawn wagons. Most who could, walked alongside their animals. The fact that people could actually walk the distance made a new mode of transportation viable—handcarts.

The design of a lighter vehicle resulted in a small wagon box three or four feet long with side and end pieces about eight inches high. These handcarts resembled carts used by porters and street sweepers in the cities of the United States. Directions on how to construct a handcart were precise and included exact woods to be used in the building of each part: hickory for axle trees, red or slippery elm for hubs, white oak for spokes and wheel rims, white ash for fills or shafts and for making the cribs or beds that would hold all of the belongings to be moved. The handcart companies were instructed to bring only a change of clothing, their tools, design patterns, and trade publications. Food for an entire company was carried in ox-drawn supply wagons. The old and infirm were also transported in the supply wagons.

The majority of the people in the handcart companies were urban

English and Scandinavians. The three thousand emigrants pulling and pushing the 653 carts for over a thousand miles endured an exacting ordeal of their bodies and spirits. It took consecrated resolution and the sustaining conviction of a deeply religious faith to make the trip. The old, the babies, and the children who died on the trail—no matter what method of transportation was employed—made each pioneer aware of the challenge of survival in the bitterest circumstances of weather, breakdown, and weariness.

According to directions, the eight companies that left the Missouri River in early summer came through successfully without undue casualties. They out-traveled the ox teams so that some complained of being slowed down by the accompanying wagons. However, two late companies, caught in the unfortunate combination of a late start and an early winter, suffered a terrible loss of life.

Mormon journals abound with stories such as that of twenty-six-year-old Elizabeth Parkes from Derby, England. She was emigrating to be with her sisters in Utah and was unfortunate to be traveling in one of the late handcart companies, the Edward Martin Company. They were trapped by unseasonable snow and cold with inadequate food and clothing. Many died and were crippled from frostbitten hands and feet. Food supplies ran low, and hunger was rampant.

A large relief effort was mounted from Salt Lake City and surrounding towns, but the ox-drawn relief wagons made slow progress in the vast, snow-covered wilderness of Utah and Wyoming. All those saved were close to death, and most could not walk.[22]

Elizabeth Parkes' sisters, Jemima and Annie, lived in Salt Lake City where they worked for Brigham Young. The sisters searched the returning wagons carrying the survivors of the Edward Martin Company. When Jemima located Elizabeth, she asked, "Lizzie can you walk?" Her sister replied with characteristic pioneer spunk, "Yes, I've had plenty of practice and am quite good at it." She was taken into the Lion House, one of Brigham Young's homes, where she was nursed back to health by Young's wives and her own sisters. Elizabeth worked for the Brigham Young household for several years until she married Thomas Higgs, one of the many English carpenters and cabinetmakers Young employed to help build and furnish his homes.[23] (figures 1.18, 1.19)

THE FIRST DECADE IN DESERET WILDERNESS CHALLENGED CRAFTSMEN AND OTHER SETTLERS

The first decade in the Utah Territory was precarious for the cabinetmakers and their families as well as for all other people. Everyone had many jobs and had to use multiple skills. But the opportunities offered by the cooperative Mormon society meant there was hope that life would become much better for these craftsmen than the one they had left behind in Europe and England.

The years 1857–58 were an especially fearful time for the Mormons because thirty thousand of those living in northern Utah were forced to abandon their crops and flee persecution. They moved to southern Utah, where they lived in wagons and dugouts as they had when immigrating.

President James Buchanan sent fifteen thousand U.S. Army soldiers to take control of the Utah Territory from the Mormons. He appointed Alfred Cumming of Georgia as the new governor to replace Brigham Young. Because the Mormon people were not in rebellion, peaceful negotiations solved the misunderstandings. The unnecessary persecution by the federal government nevertheless damaged relations with the non-Mormon community. Referred to by the Mormons as *gentiles*, these non-Mormons showed no support for Brigham Young nor their Mormon neighbors during the three-year occupation. The resulting division affected business between the two groups for the remainder of the nineteenth century. Cooperatives for commerce became important to ensure the economic survival of the Mormons. These cooperatives are discussed at length in chapter four.

The U.S. Army, stationed at Camp Floyd, pulled out when the soldiers were needed to fight in the Civil War. The vast array of materials they left behind benefited all the people of Utah.[24]

In the fall of 1860, the church announced a new method of travel for converts. In lieu of handcarts, ox-drawn wagons were sent from Salt Lake City to the Missouri River to pick up waiting converts and prearranged

FIGURE 1.19

KITCHEN, BEEHIVE HOUSE
Variety of makers
One of many residences of Brigham Young
  and his family
Collection at Beehive House, LDS Church

wagons. The knowledgeable drivers efficiently transported the immigrants and goods from the East back to Salt Lake City, and then in the same season, went back to the Missouri River to meet the next group that would travel in the spring. The last mass-immigration years from 1864 to 1868 brought 9,264 people to Utah. The church's train system became one of the most successfully organized emigration systems in the history of the United States during the nineteenth century.[25]

Importing of goods increased, and people were able to begin living at a higher level of comfort and style. Furniture and stylebooks arrived. The beginning of the taste in Victorian revival, Rococo, Gothic, Elizabethan, and Renaissance styles that were popular in eastern American cities were the newest designs created by the outstanding craftsmen in Utah. (figures 1.20, 1.21, 1.22, 1.23)

Pioneering in different areas of Utah lasted for at least forty years after the first pioneers arrived, because new communities were being settled all the time. New towns were also begun long after the railroad came in 1869. Working the land was difficult, and no settler had an easy time. But ingenuity and diligent work started paying off by the 1870s.

Carpenters and master cabinetmakers, who were in great demand, were willing to set up workshops in new communities because of their belief in establishing an outstanding culture throughout Zion. Scandinavian and English cabinetmakers worked as the principal craftsmen, making furniture in many areas of the territory long after the Americans of the same trade listed themselves as carpenters and built homes and other buildings.

Brigham Young assumed the leadership for excellent craftsmanship, and his encouragement reflected the goals espoused by the ideal society they were attempting to create. The census lists an increasing number of cabinetmakers until 1869, when the transcontinental railroad joined Utah to all the material culture of both coasts. The twenty-three Utah cabinetmakers, who were already working in multiple occupations, found the competition tough. This was also a period of tremendous production with a variety of furniture designs by American and English craftsmen. Even though the furniture designs varied, an attitude of simple refinement pervaded. Locally made and imported furniture pieces were generally more simple in design

FIGURE 1.20

FLOUR SAFE
Anonymous maker
Pine, painted and grained, faux oak and
   mahogany
46 x 42 x 20 in.
Collection of LDS Church

FIGURE 1.21

RECTILINEAR BED
Anonymous maker
Pine four-poster, spooled, turned,
  crotch grained
48 x 51 in.
Collection of Gwen Wilcox at Pioneer
  Trail State Park

with few exceptions. Materials still affected proportions, and the local pine never could be fashioned with as fine or light proportions as the hardwoods. Painted surfaces could be delightful, but the ease of maintenance and durability made the harder woods still more desirable.

Understanding the challenges, attitudes, and supreme efforts the Mormon pioneers made in establishing their goal of an ideal, refined, Christian society in a difficult, mountainous desert is critical in understanding the individual pieces of their remaining furniture. Styles brought by craftsmen and the adaptation to materials they found in the desert and mountain areas caused new proportions, new designs, and new surface treatments.

The assimilation of diverse people demanded that their various traditions and material cultures be combined with new necessities for survival in the wilderness. These factors gave the people different perspectives about the traditional furniture designs of their experience and the new styles they admired.

The Utah Territory was built by an industrious religious people who were willing to live in isolated communities separated by vast distances. They struggled against deprivation of water, extreme climate, plagues, limited supplies, and limited world help or understanding. They succeeded against these challenges in creating a unique and ideal Christian society.

FIGURE 1.22

BED
Anonymous maker
Pine
Erastus Bingham Cabin, North Ogden
Headboard: 50 x 48 in.
Footboard: 32 x 48 in.
Collection of Lagoon Corporation

FIGURE 1.23

KITCHEN, COVE FORT
Variety of makers
Spooled backs and legs on chairs,
  tables, benches
Folding side on table, fiddle-back and
  rod-back chairs
Collection of Cove Fort

NOTES

1. Oscar P. Fitzgerald, *Three Centuries of American Furniture* (Prentice Hall, 1982), 109–32.

2. L. R. Arrington, *Great Basin Kingdom* (University of Utah Press, 1958), 1–34.

3. See note 2 above.

4. *History of the Church* 7:464.

5. See note 4 above.

6. B. B. Smith, Autobiography from *Journals of Bathsheba Bigler Smith*, LDS Archives, 14.

7. Peter Wilson Cownover, *Journal* (Utah State Historical Society), 4–9.

8. See note 6 above.

9. *History of Nauvoo*, LDS Archives.

10. See note 7 above.

11. William Clayton, *Journal.*

12. See note 2 above.

13. See note 4 above.

14. Lydia Ann Seeley Cownover, *History for 1892, Cornerstone of Brigham Young Academy.*

15. L. R. Arrington, *Great Basin Kingdom*, 98–99; and A. Hafen, *Handcarts to Zion* (University of Nebraska Press, 1960) 27–54.

16. K. F. Brough, *Freely I Gave, History and Journal of Jacob G. Bigler* (Utah State Historical Society), 38.

17. Mathew W. Dalton, Biography taken from the oral histories and diaries of Mathew W. Dalton, Family of Mathew Dalton, 39.

18. Utah State Arts Council, *Our Company's Heritage*, 34.

19. *Millennial Star*, Liverpool, England, X 1848, 81–88.

20. J. Hulmston, *Utah Historical Quarterly*, 58, no. 1:33–48.

21. Charles Dickens, *The Uncommercial Traveler* (New York: Oxford University Press, 1958), 220–32.

22. See note 15 above, 194.

23. D. Higgs Smith, *Parkes Family History*, 26–27.

24. See note 15 above.

25. Utah Census 1850, 1870, 1880.

THE DESERT BLOOMS

✳   ✳   ✳

The establishment of a Latter-day Saint furniture style in the wilderness of the Utah Territory is best appreciated with a brief overview of furniture pieces and styles before exploring craftsmen region by region. Examples of fashionable and functional Mormon furniture are varied in style for two major reasons: the diverse backgrounds of their makers, and the constraints of their limited material resources. Pieces were occasionally created in hardwood, often of packing-box parts, and most often of the softer conifer woods available in the wilderness environments. The ingenuity, skill, and creative style imposed upon inferior materials by artisans who most often had only hand tools for crafting, is nowhere better understood than through a review of the basic piece of pioneer furniture— the chair.

CHAIR DESIGNS COMMON TO EARLY MORMON MAKERS AND PIONEER HOMES

Slat-back chair with or without arms

This chair featuring multiple horizontal rails was important in all states, with variations called *ladder-back*, *Shaker*, and *Creole*.

Seat varieties included woven rush, wood slat, and woven or stretched leathers.

Woods selected for this chair style were commonly maple, hickory, or ash, because a thin, strong rail derived from those hardwoods adequately supported weight while being able to be lathe-turned or carved to a more delicate line.

FIGURE 2.1

ROD-BACK CHAIR
Seeley Owen
Pine, painted and grained, faux mahogany
26 x 14½ in.
Seat height: 14 in.
Collection of great-granddaughter
  Mrs. Elizabeth Conover Reynolds

FIGURE 2.2

LADDER-BACK CHAIR
Brigham Young
Solid hickory, stenciled, painted, rush seat
32 x 18 in.
Seat height: 15 in.
Collection of LDS Church

FIGURE 2.3

Wagon train in 1866, with pioneer rod-back
and slat-back chairs in the wagon.
LDS Church Archives
Photo: Charles William Carter

Though many of these chairs were transported to the new settlements, *slat-back chairs* made in Utah of local pine were heavier, with heartier leg turnings required of the softer conifer wood to support enough weight to match the capabilities of hardwood chairs in similar styles.

Windsor chairs

The *Windsor-style* chair was of English design origin, dating from the sixteenth century. The Windsor style was first crafted in America in 1725 and was known throughout the colonies before the Revolutionary War. The style became identified with that war period.

With the influence of Empire and Victorian taste in America, furniture styles became more elaborate. The *Sheraton fancy chair* replaced the Windsor in popularity, and by 1850, the handmade Windsor was out of style. Factory-made versions remained popular for many years. The rod-back and the low-back were the most popular.

The low-back *captain's chair*, known to Mormons as the *Congress chair*, was an adaptation of the eighteenth-century, low-back Windsor.

The seat of a well-made Windsor was constructed from softwood without knots. It is important to note that Utah pine was low in resins, and as the growth cycles were determined by arid conditions, the knots were small and the wood lightweight. Pine seats were well shaped and hollowed out to fit the shape of the average person for maximum comfort while providing a chair material that, though heavier in appearance than hardwood, was not unduly heavy.

Spindles and legs were constructed from hardwoods—such as hickory, white oak, ash, or maple—that would be less likely to split or splinter and yet be capable of holding more weight.

FIGURE 2.4

DIXIE ROCKER
Anonymous maker
Pine, grained
41 x 27 in.
Seat height: 21 in.
Rockers: 37 in.
Collection of Pioneer Trail State Park

The Windsor chair was known in all East Coast states and in Missouri, Illinois, Ohio, and Nebraska where Mormon settlements were located. Variations of the chair style in all of those areas are defined by the locally available wood and are unique to the individual craftsman's concepts and skills.

Nineteenth-century Windsor chairs were heavier and clumsier of line than the eighteenth-century ones. The most popular Windsor styles during the nineteenth century in Utah were the *rod-back* and the *low-back* chairs. Windsor furniture included rockers, children's chairs, infant high chairs, cradles, and settees. The *Boston rocker* is a Windsor design. The Mormon pine version is heavier but is essentially the same rocker. Such rockers made in southern Utah were known as *Dixie rockers*. The Boston-rocker style is recognized by its rolled seat and arms, extended rockers, and often stenciled embellishments. The back of the chair typically had seven to nine spindles and a conventional scroll back. (figure 2.4)

The little Boston rocking chair had five spindles, no arms, and was called the *nursing chair* or *nurse rocker*.

FIGURE 2.5

FIDDLEBACK CHAIR
Anonymous maker
Pine, regrained and detailed
32 x 14 in.
Seat height: 15½ in.
Collection of Richard Blanck

Fiddleback chairs

Fiddleback chairs were an adaptation of a *Queen Anne style*. They are identified primarily by their vase-shaped or fiddle-shaped back splat. The *fiddleback Boston rocker* is a very late version of this style and is considered Midwestern, made predominantly of hardwood in Ohio and Indiana. (figure 2.5)

Fiddleback rockers fashioned in Utah were made of pine, with the style adapted to the softwood and appearing heavier in design. All were painted, and most were grained or stenciled.

Sheraton chairs

Sheraton chair styles evolved from the formal styles of the eighteenth century in England, particularly from the parlor and dining room, where guests were entertained.

Sheraton fancy chairs were popular in New York by 1797. These chairs were painted rather than crafted of fine, hand-rubbed hardwoods, so that the colonists could afford them. During the nineteenth century, fancy chairs were mass-produced. They were especially popular in river communities. The *Hitchcock chair* style became fashionable in the Midwest. The term *Hitchcock* is a generic term meaning "any painted chair made during the nineteenth century," but the true Hitchcock chair is signed by the factory of Lambert Hitchcock and marked "L. Hitchcock, Hitchcocksville, Connecticut. Warranted."

Many Sheraton fancy chairs were sold in Utah, and one very ingenious chair maker family—the Thomas Cottam family—made unique Sheraton fancy chairs. These chair makers were from England and produced fancy chairs in a beautiful mix of Yorkshire and East Anglia English styles.

Sheraton chairs consisted of a variety of turned parts that were made on a lathe. The parts were unique to the chair maker and may be documented by particular styles. They were formal or very informal according to the painting and stenciling, the patterns cut out in the horizontal rails, and the leg and rail turnings. Seats on Sheraton chairs were usually woven of rush or made of wood plank. (figures 2.6, 2.31)

Slat-back chairs

Fancy slat-back chairs were produced in Brigham Young's cabinet shop in Nauvoo, Illinois. Producing those chairs for sale supported Young's family while he served a mission to England. It is conjecture whether Young actually made fancy chairs later on as he did other chairs and furniture, but there is no doubt that his commissions for chairs of certain styles to particular craftsmen influenced other makers. His involvement in designs and finishing techniques is verifiable.

Empire chairs

The most influential chair ever built was the *Klismos chair*, which inspired many adaptations in the neoclassical style. The popular *Empire gondola chair* was one of several nineteenth-century chairs inspired by the Klismos chair depicted on ancient Greek vases.

Mormon Empire gondola chairs were unique because they were made of pine with a Windsor-shaped seat and turned legs that were shorter than the European versions that had inspired them. The chair was painted and grained to look like hardwood.

The Empire gondola was made in the Public Works shop, where the wages were paid in scrip that could be redeemed at the tithing warehouse for most of the necessities of life.

Some of the Empire gondola chairs produced in the Public Works cabinet shop have a brand that reads "*Public Works/G.S.L.C.*" (figures 2.9, 2.10)

It is helpful to also be aware of the breadth of design in other basic pieces of furniture created by pioneer Mormon craftsmen during the colonization period. Beds, tables, and the versatile lounges were designed and built from wagon parts and local woods as the immigrants were called by the church to move from place to place. In the settlement process, craftsmen were always sent with the first groups to prepare the way with buildings and furniture for their families and those who followed.

Beds

Early beds had lacings or ropes that held the mattresses in place. Later beds, built from about 1860, had wood slats to support the mattresses. Most beds were designed with the lacing or rope mattress-support style.

FIGURE 2.6

SHERATON ROCKER
John Cottam
Pine, painted and grained, faux mahogany
43 x 21½ in.
Seat height: 15 in.
Collection of Pioneer Trail State Park

Two basic bed shapes are high post and low post, with the majority of beds having been produced in the low-post design.

Spooled, or *Jenny Lind*, *beds* were found in Utah. These beds were usually made from pine, maple, or birch and had painted surface treatments. They had wooden slats to hold the mattress in place and often had trundle beds that rolled under the main bed.

Rounded corners on these Jenny Lind beds came after 1850, when furniture-makers developed methods of bending the spool turnings.

Lounges

Lounges were a common sturdy piece of furniture popular during the nineteenth century in Canada, northeastern America, and Utah. They were important because their serviceability made them useful for large families, visitors, and gathering places. Myth and story have named the lounge the *Mormon couch*, but it is not unique to the Mormon culture. The great number of them, and their individuality, made them a worthy style of Americana. These lounges were typically the size and width of a single bed. The principle of making the lounge into a bed was simple but ingenious: alternating wood slats in the platform could be pulled out to accommodate a second person. Extending the base in this manner afforded a versatile piece of furniture that functioned both as a fairly comfortable seating piece and a simple bed. This practical versatility appealed to the Mormon people. The shape and size of the couches was fairly standard, but variations occurred as individual cabinetmakers, turners, and commissioning customers made their personal adjustments to style and size. A surprising number of the lounges photographed for this book were only single-bed size, with no adjustment provided for expanding to a larger width. (figures 4.5–.11)

Pedestal tables

Pedestal tables were popular and were often preserved in better condition than other pieces because they were used in the parlor or as the table where the family gathered for scripture study and pleasure reading.

All of the major cabinetmakers made large pedestal tables, generally of pine, painted or grained to look like exotic woods. They also made small pedestal tables with lathe-turned bases. The apron on the table was generally detailed in some manner, sometimes with an elongated curve or occasionally with carving. The octagon-shaped pedestal table was a great favorite of English convert and cabinetmaker William Bell. He grained his pedestal tables to resemble the finest walnut and mahogany hardwoods.

Ralph Ramsay's pedestal bases were turned from a large piece of wood, with smaller pieces carved and applied to give the base a sculptured appearance and his personal identity of style. His tables were painted and grained to resemble walnut or high-style—and expensive—rosewood. (figure 2.7)

Drop-leaf tables

Drop-leaf tables were popular with Mormon immigrants, especially the Scandinavians. Their artisans grained and painted such tables in a high-style manner suitable for formal parlors. The very elegant crotch-mahogany finish was a great favorite and difficult to execute believably.

Both drop-leaf tables and harvest tables were built from packing boxes and parts of the wagons that had made the journey to Utah. Table legs were generally constructed of turned pine.

The rococo revival taste and the *Eastlake tables* imported from Europe didn't become important until after the completion of the transcontinental railroad. Eastlake style became the most popular, and Eastern furniture makers sold large numbers of such tables in the 1870s–'80s.

FIGURE 2.7

PEDESTAL TABLE
Ralph Ramsay, during his Richfield period
Empire scroll elements, foot and table
   support
Pine, carved and applied pieces,
   inlay on apron
30 x 43 (diameter) in.
Collection of Mr. & Mrs. D. J. Barker Jr.

Unlike the leaders of many colonizing groups throughout history who imposed their tastes on followers and conquered peoples, Brigham Young was more than an inspirational mentor in matters of taste as well as spiritual and temporal encouragement; he excelled in personal skills with his hands and his mind. Where other builders of empires through the millennia have been warriors or wealthy people with visions of power, Brigham Young wanted to create spiritual and material plenty for everyone. His goals in both areas came from his devout belief in the highest level of execution possible to one's ability and the collective ability of the group.

Brigham Young is considered one of America's great colonizers by historians within and outside of The Church of Jesus Christ of Latter-day Saints. His spiritual and colonizing leadership is recognized by church members and historians as critical to the survival and growth of the people and the religion. His public encouragement to create a society of culture, and his commitment to the fine arts make Brigham Young unique among state-builders and chroniclers in the history of the nation. Fine craftsmanship in wood was among the arts he supported out of his own background as a cabinetmaker of great skill.

In a letter dated 19 February 1876, to George Hickox, an acquaintance from Young's New York days, he wrote:

> *I felt amused and interested in your statement that a chair made by me would occupy a place in your Centennial supper to be held next Tuesday. I have no doubt that many other pieces of furniture and other specimens of my handiwork can be found scattered about your section of the country, for I have believed all of my life that, that which was worth doing was worth doing well, and have considered it as much a part of religion to do honest, reliable work, such as would endure, for those who employed me, as to attend to the services of God's worship on the Sabbath.*[1]

Raised in Vermont, Brigham Young's cabinetmaking experience had begun during the spring of 1817–18 when, at age sixteen, he had become independent. He bound himself out to various families in and around Auburn, New York, for his room and a small stipend. He was apprenticed to John C. Jeffries, who advertised "Chair Making, Sign Painting and Gilding" in the local newspaper. In the *Paper Advocate of the People*, in Auburn on 28 May 1817, Jeffries advertised, "All kinds of chairs, well finished and neatly painted, on hand for sale as usual." As his apprentice, Brigham Young learned the trades of carpenter, painter, and glazier. He recalled of that experience:

FIGURE 2.8

CHEST OF DRAWERS
Brigham Young
Solid walnut
Turned knobs and feet
Carved, lower side panels
67 x 37 x 21 in.
Collection of LDS Church
Photo: Jed Clark

*The first job my boss gave me was to make a bedstead out of an old log that
had been on the beach of the lake for years, water-logged and watersoaked.
Said he—"There are tools, you cut that log into right lengths for a bedstead.
Hew out the side rails, the end rails and the posts; get a board for a head
board, and go to work and make a bedstead." And I went to work and cut up
the log, split it up to the best of my ability, and made a bedstead that, I
suppose they used for many years. I would go to work and learn to make a
washboard, and make a bench to put the wash tub on, and to make a chair.[2]*

One of Young's early assignments as Jeffries' assistant was to do the
painting in the home of Judge Elijah Miller, a cultured and important man.
His tastes were for high-style formality. His daughter married William
Seward, who later became the governor of New York and secretary of state
under Presidents Abraham Lincoln and Andrew Johnson. This house is a
fine museum today, boasting an ornate mantelpiece reputed to be the work
of Brigham Young. Young also worked on the Brown house across the street,
and in the winter months produced a supply of beautifully handcrafted
mantelpieces and sold them to other local carpenters. Many people in that
area claim to have a mantelpiece made by Brigham Young.[3]

Years later, in a sermon to his Mormon followers, Young summed up
those years in New York as a cabinetmaker and carpenter:

*Among various other occupations I have been a carpenter, painter and glazier,
and when I learned my trades and worked, both as journeyman and master,
if I took a job of painting and glazing, say to the amount of one pound
sterling, or five dollars, and through my own carelessness in any manner
injured the work or material, I considered it my duty to repair the injury at
my own expense.[4]*

Young took pride in his trade and pleasure in assisting others with his
knowledge and occasionally with his skill. After he became prophet and
head of the Mormon Church and governor of the Utah Territory, he still
relied on his occupational knowledge when making commissions and giving
directives to the craftsmen building temples and church offices.

Young understood the unique differences between craftsmen, how to
achieve good design, and where to assign cabinetmakers to establish a particular culture. The challenge of creating a genteel society in the desert of the
Rocky Mountains was successful because of his practical and knowledgeable
leadership, for Young had designed, copied, and cataloged in his mind the
best of furniture and carpentry designs. He recognized the English and
European apprentice systems as being close to what he had experienced and
knew the quality of work that could be accomplished by a master. The steps

FIGURE 2.9

TWO GONDOLA CHAIRS
William Bell
One signed William Bell, one stamped
  Public Works
Both a standard Public Works Empire
  gondola size specification
33 x 15 in.
Seat height: 17 in.
Collection of Lagoon Corporation

FIGURE 2.10

PUBLIC WORKS STAMP
Collection of LDS Church, Lagoon
  Corporation

of apprenticeship trained a cabinetmaker to make a practical and fashionable piece of furniture.

Brigham Young knew what current designs were fashionable in England because he had served a mission there. In America, where New York had become the leading city in setting furniture-design style, Duncan Phyfe designs had created a furor of excitement that spread to Europe and beyond. Young was also aware of the Hitchcock chair factories and had worked in the furniture factory of Colonel John Richardson in Auburn.

Becoming familiar with the new inventions in the furniture-making industry was a pleasurable part of Young's life on the eastern seaboard. Later, as he was establishing Zion in the land of Deseret, he insisted that the newest tools, techniques, and designs be used in laying the groundwork for the culture of the Mormons.

The Public Works organization of the church gave work to tradesmen immediately upon their entering the Salt Lake Valley. Unquestionably, the factory method of furniture manufacturing was sponsored and encouraged by Young. He gave his ideas to the builders of chairs and other furniture being made there and was critically important to the Public Works factory, in which he took great pride. In fact, President Young gave each of his sons a Mormon Empire gondola chair from the factory, inscribed with their names. (figures 2.9, 2.10)

Presenting gifts of furniture to his children, grandchildren, and close friends was a rule with him, not an exception. Several of the furniture pieces had been constructed from the boxes that he used to make the first trip into the valley of the Great Salt Lake. Most of his finer gifts of furniture were made by William Bell, Ralph Ramsay, or John and Thomas Cottam. Young purchased furniture from other cabinetmakers, but these four Englishmen were craftsmen whom he personally sponsored.

Bell, Ramsay, and the Cottams were so influential in imprinting their own styles upon the designs of what became known as Mormon furniture, that they will be introduced here. In later chapters, other outstanding furniture craftsmen will be discussed in turn by the regions where their cabinet shops were located.

WILLIAM BELL

William Bell had a great influence on high-quality craftsmanship in architectural embellishment and furniture design produced in Salt Lake City from 1854, when he arrived with the James Brown Company of immigrants, to 1869, when he went on a mission in Heber City, Utah, where he established a cabinet shop.

FIGURE 2.11

OCTAGONAL TABLE
William Bell
Empire elements, scroll foot design
Inlay patterns
Made from packing boxes from the first-
  company wagons of Brigham Young
  and Lorenzo Snow
27 x 36 (diameter) in.
Collection of Salt Lake City DUP

Working exclusively for his patron Brigham Young, Bell's outstanding craftsmanship was utilized to its fullest potential. He lived in President Young's first home, The White House, and worked in Young's cabinet shop. His own shop was built sometime before 1859. Records place him as the owner of the property on the southeast corner of Brigham Young's land, where the president was a frequent shop visitor.

Bell had been involved in the cabinetmaking business from his childhood, when he had been taken out of school to assist his carpenter father. He progressed through the journeyman ranks necessary to become a master cabinetmaker. In 1833, he moved to London, where he had a successful business until 1854. At that time, he and his wife emigrated to America and traversed west, arriving in Utah on 1 October 1854.

It was on seeing his furniture-building and carving skill that Brigham Young immediately set Bell to the task of designing and executing furniture for his own homes, and designing pieces to be created by the Public Works business for other projects. Furniture from Public Works, especially chairs, are attributed to both Brigham Young and William Bell at the same time. Both men were skilled at structural as well as painting and graining techniques. The origin of some Public Works pieces in the Latter-day Saint archives remains a mystery. (figures 2.11, 2.12)

Once established in Utah, Bell had the time and the workshop to produce furniture. Though President Young was busy throughout the Utah Territory at many levels of the colonization process, he loved his past trade and involved himself in the design and production of new furniture. Though undocumented, it is presumed he may have grained and glazed a piece or two personally.

It is unique in the history of the American furniture industry that a powerful and professionally trained patron partnered with a skilled and knowledgeable craftsman to execute exceptional designs before they were known or accepted in the established urban style centers of the nation.

Making furniture for Young apparently kept Bell busy, but there are three documented instances of his involvement with other cabinetmakers. Though he supplied Brigham Young's households and supervised the Public Works furniture shop, he belonged to the Dinwoodey Association of craftsmen for the maintenance of high standards, discussed in chapter four.

In 1855, J. C. Little noted that his Deseret Carriage and Furniture Depot had "just formed a connection with . . . William Bell, recently from London, the best and most experienced cabinetmaker and upholsterer in the Territory." Bell was a member of the furniture-awarding committee of the

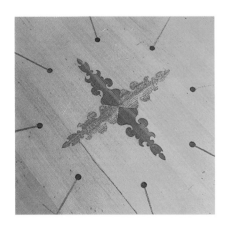

FIGURE 2.12

Detail, octagonal table (figure 2.11)

FIGURE 2.13

RECLINING CHAIR
William Bell
Pine, tufted leather
Made for Brigham Young
46 x 23 in.
Seat height: 20 in.
Collection of John Told

Annual Fair of the Deseret Agricultural and Manufacturing Society (D. A. & M.) in 1861. He entered the contest and won $3 for the best rocking chair.

William Bell was part of the exciting group of English craftsmen who were creating a fashionable new culture in the Rocky Mountain desert. This group had left off producing the latest styles in England to execute them six months later in Utah, just as the Mormon people were emerging from their precarious survival existence and establishing homes of consequence. They demanded the newest fashion while also desiring simplicity. Bell's designs fit those criteria. His furniture lines were simple, elegant, and refined, but neither stark nor ostentatious. He worked in Empire and several Victorian styles, especially the Gothic Victorian, graining pine pieces to resemble walnut and mahogany. Bell even experimented with new mechanical furniture parts and made at least two reclining chairs years before a U.S. patent was recorded. (figure 2.13)

An outstanding example of unique design, construction, and graining is Bell's design for the octagonal, rotating, tithing desks used in Brigham Young's office and the church tithing office. The graining, attributed to Brigham Young, exquisitely simulates wood, marble, and leather. (figure 2.15)

FIGURE 2.14

DESK
William Bell maker, Ralph Ramsay carver
Brigham Young used this desk in his office
Drop-leaf desk
Pine, grained, faux oak, turned octagonal legs
Table: 28 x 59 x 33 in.
Desk leaf: 24 x 18 x 57 in.
Collection of LDS Church, Beehive House

FIGURE 2.15

OCTAGONAL DESK
William Bell
Pine, painted and grained, faux marble,
    leather, and mahogany, attributed to
    Brigham Young
Unique revolving desk
44 x 82 (diameter) in.
Collection of LDS Church

William Bell and fellow Englishman Ralph Ramsay created many unique woodcraft projects in Bell's shop, the most notable of which is the eagle with an eleven-foot wingspan. This sculpture was used to crown the entrance gate to Brigham Young's Salt Lake City property. Record of the eagle being installed on the gate in 1859 affirms both the activity and the spatial capabilities of Bell's shop at that time.

On 6 January 1859, Brigham Young gave his guests a tour of his Lion House parlor, proudly encouraging them to examine tables of superb workmanship made by William Bell. The tables were made of mahogany from a log given as a gift to President Young by misters Williams and Hooper. Such imported hardwood logs were highly prized in Utah.

Bell was proficient in executing pieces of furniture from hardwoods; his marquetry shows that he understood many types of hard- and softwoods. (figures 2.11, 2.12)

Bell also served a mission in 1869 to an area presided over by his friend and customer Heber C. Kimball. His calling was to teach and to establish a fine-furniture workshop for Heber and Utah Valley. An entry in the *History of Heber City* notes, "Early carpenters such as William Bell, George Blackley and Henry McMullin made the first wooden coffins." Bell built furniture in the Heber area until three years before his death in 1886.[5]

FIGURE 2.18

PEDESTAL TABLE
William Bell and Ralph Ramsay
Pine, painted and grained, faux rosewood
High-style carving
30 x 42 (diameter) in.
Collection of Richard Blanck

RALPH RAMSAY

In the nineteenth century, furniture technology was dependent upon available woods and talent that could combine the practical function of a piece with original design and outstanding craftsmanship. Pioneer Mormon furniture makers who could achieve that level in their craft were held in high esteem, and today their furniture is regarded as priceless.

Born 22 January 1824 near Ryton, in the County of Durham, England, Ralph Ramsay served his cabinetmaking apprenticeship through the journeyman and master levels in his native country. He succeeded well in his fifteen-year career there in the trades of cabinetmaker, wood-turner, and wood-carver. He had been a Mormon for seven years and had lost his wife Emma Clark and their child, Joseph, when he married Elizabeth Burns before emigrating to Salt Lake City with the Daniel D. McArthur Handcart Company on 26 September 1856.

Once settled in Utah, Ramsay reported that he lived with a Bell family and collaborated with William Bell, the cabinetmaker. Even though Bell and Ramsay were from different parts of England, their steps of apprenticeship had been the same. They collaborated many times, often on the same piece of furniture.

During the eighteen years he lived in Salt Lake City, Ramsay was given jobs of significance from Brigham Young because of his originality and versatility in wood. Young's sponsorship resulted in major designs and commissions that became symbolic of Mormon culture.

FIGURE 2.19

DETAIL MOLDINGS
Ralph Ramsay
Carved for William Jennings residence
Photo: Utah State Historical Society

FIGURE 2.20

WILLIAM JENNINGS HOME
[Now the Devereau House]
A high-style Mormon home
Photo: Utah State Historical Society

Eagles and beehives became Ramsay's specialties, and his carvings of them and other themes are particularly noteworthy. President Young hired him to help build and beautify the Beehive House, and requested of him many furniture commissions, though the majority of the furniture in Brigham's several homes was done by William Bell. (figures 2.25, 2.26)

Two different accounts tell of Ralph Ramsay's workshops and business specialties. Joseph Openshaw recalled Ramsay's workshop by City Creek in Salt Lake City:

> *Our house was within about two rods of the creek that carried water to the water wheel that turned the planing mill and the saws and other things such as a carding machine and turning lathe that Ralph Ramsay had there, and also an iron lathe that Mr. Tremain used to turn all of the shafts or any iron thing that had to be made round, or holes that had to be made in iron that was too large for a bit. Mr. Ramsay turned all kinds of wooden things, such as chair legs and table legs. He also turned the posts that hold up the gallery in the Tabernacle. After he had gotten them turned, he had to bore a 2½-inch hole in the center of each post the full length, to stop it from cracking, then carved ornaments for the top of the post. He was surely an artist. We children used to watch him do these things and sometimes we could get him to make us a top, as it would only take him two or three minutes to make one. He also made the eagle for the Eagle Gate.[6] (figure 2.22)*

FIGURE 2.21

DETAIL, ORNATE CARVING
Ralph Ramsay
Cornice work, William Jennings residence
Photo: Utah State Historical Society

FIGURE 2.22

EAGLE GATE
Ralph Ramsay
Original gate to Brigham Young's property
Hand carved, eleven-foot wingspan
Five pieces of wood
Photo: Utah State Historical Society

FIGURE 2.23

MANTELPIECE
Ralph Ramsay
Fireplace of the Richfield home of
 Ralph Ramsay
Pine, hand carved, painted and grained,
 faux oak
Collection of the Ralph Ramsay Home,
 National Historic Register

A *Deseret News* notice of 16 August 1863 read:

> *Ralph Ramsay, WOOD CARVER AND TURNER, having fitted up machinery in the house lately occupied by President B. Young's Wood-Carving machine on the City Creek, is now prepared to execute all kinds of Carving and Turning. Columns for Porticoes, Verandahs, Halls, Galleries, etc. Turned and Carved to order. Country orders attended to R. Ramsay, 20th Ward, G.S.L. City.*[7]

Ramsay carved the eagle that topped the entrance gate to Brigham Young's property in William Bell's workshop, located near his home. When he spoke to a reporter from the *Deseret News* regarding his career as a tradesman, he said,

> *While the Eagle Gate may furnish the most notable piece of work I did, it was the least of my carving. But as to that old bird, I am proud to say that I carved every curve of its body. It is my work from beginning to end. I want to say this much for the reason that is has been stated that someone else had a hand in it. Don't forget that I did all of it, every whit. Put that down my boy, it is mine, all mine!*[8]

The eleven-foot wingspan of the eagle required five blocks of wood: one for the body, another for the neck, two for the wings, and the fifth for the beehive mounting. He selected the wood for it from the gallery of trees growing along City Creek. The actual eagle used as the model for the carved eagle was one that had been killed by Truman Angell, the church architect. (figure 2.22)

Ramsay also carved the wooden oxen that became the models for the cast figures supporting baptismal fonts in Mormon temples. He built the elaborate casework of the Salt Lake Tabernacle organ, the

FIGURE 2.24

BEEHIVE BUFFET
Attributed to Ralph Ramsay, Brigham
  Young's gift to Hyrum B. Clawson
Made from wood saved from the Mormon
  Tabernacle organ
60 x 24 x 71 in.
Owned by the Young and Clawson family
  for generations
Collection of Mr. & Mrs. Eastman Hatch

ornate woodwork in the old Salt Lake Theatre, and the woodwork and furniture for the Beehive and Lion Houses of Brigham Young. Ramsay's mantelpiece won first place as the best specimen of wood carving exhibited at the D. A. & M. Fair in 1860. (figures 2.22, 2.23)

The requirements of some of his work forced Ramsay to put together small pieces in order to create sculptured objects or large-dimension furniture.

He was as remarkable a gatherer and assembler of wood as he was a carver of difficult-to-obtain materials. As with other craftsmen, wood remained a significant challenge to Ramsay, who worked with the available timber where he lived. His favorite wood types were quaking aspen, red cedar (red pine), and black walnut. However, examples of his furniture abound in yellow pine, cottonwood, black willow, and mountain mahogany.

Even the most utilitarian of pieces he created were traceable in their elegance to the classical furniture style in fashion in England and to his training in the carving art at Newcastle-on-Tyne.

FIGURE 2.25

HALL TREE
Ralph Ramsay and William Bell
Commissioned by Brigham Young
Mountain mahogany
91 x 37 in.
Collection of Salt Lake City DUP

FIGURE 2.26

Detail, hall tree

FIGURE 2.27

BEDSTEAD
Ralph Ramsay
Ramsay's personal bed, begun in 1860 in
    Salt Lake City from lintels of the first
    home of Parley P. Pratt, added to for
    decades in each place he lived,
    completed in 1898
Black walnut hardwood, box elder from
    City Creek Canyon, cedar from Arizona,
    red pine and red cedar from hills of
    Richfield
Hand-carved, depicting flora and fauna of
    his various environments, and people
    showing struggle of colonization effort
    in their faces
Headboard: 82 x 53 in.
Footboard: 46 x 53 in.
Donated by son, James B. Ramsay,
    Collection of Salt Lake City DUP

FIGURE 2.28
Detail, footboard

A granddaughter described his working methods:

*Grandfather chopped, sawed by hand, sanded, polished, and carved the wood
to suit his needs. At one time his workshop was in a room of our home. It was
very interesting to watch him carve. He would hold the wood chisel in his
hand and work it with his chin. The result was that he never seemed to have
any whiskers in the middle of his chin.*[9]

Ramsay's life is best summarized as one where his devotion to the gospel
of Jesus Christ, manifested in Mormonism, was at all times the dominant
theological, social, and economic motivation for him and his family. He had
five wives in his lifetime. One died in England and he was divorced from
another. The two wives who were the mothers of his living children at that
time were important to each community in which he lived, for one was an
herbalist and doctor, and the other was a midwife and nurse.

The moving around due to hardships and church callings is reflected in
Ramsay's furniture. It is easy to attribute the carving of animals and plants
to the specific areas in which he and his family lived. The bed he carved for
himself from pieces of woods indigenous to each of the places where he
lived is truly original and personal. He worked on the bed from 1860–87,
carting it with him when he moved from Salt Lake City in 1874 to Richfield
in Sevier County, where he was a director in a cooperative movement called
the United Order. When that order dissolved, he moved his family to
St. Johns, Arizona. He lived there until 1885,
when he moved to Colonial Juarez in Chihuahua,
Old Mexico, because polygamy was outlawed by
the U.S. government. Ramsay wanted to preserve
his entire family. When laws were changed, he
moved back to Arizona in 1887 and built a home
in Snowflake, in 1891. (figures 2.27, 2.28)

The bed is covered with carvings of the
flora and fauna he observed with relocation.
There are also faces of people moved with emo-
tion, though it is less easy to identify who these
individuals were. The difficulties and sorrows
people experienced in their trials of settling a new
territory and surviving the hardships of harassment for their beliefs and practices are clearly
observable on the faces of Ramsay's bed carvings.

FIGURE 2.29

FRAME
Ralph Ramsay
Frame made to commemorate birth of
   daughter Emma, namesake of first wife
   who died in England
Hand-carved solid black walnut, mirror
   added later
Gift of Elsie Maud Frost Ramsay,
   Collection of Geraldene Ramsay Randall

Ramsay made other pieces of furniture and decorative work for family members. One of his granddaughters retained a mirror decorated with a relief portrait of his first wife, Emma, who died in England. The mirror frame was a gift for the granddaughter for whom Emma was the namesake. She said her mother told her, "Father Ramsay said he left part of his heart in England when he emigrated to America." (figure 2.29)

FIGURE 2.30

BOOKCASE DESK
Ralph Ramsay
Made by Ramsay for his Richfield home
Pine, painted and grained, faux mahogany
Fox-head drawer pulls
90½ x 24 x 14½ in.
Collection of the Ralph Ramsay Home,
   National Historic Register

John Cottam Sr. and Sons,
John Cottam Jr. and Thomas Cottam

John Cottam and his sons, John and Thomas, are listed as turners and chair makers because the term describes the majority of their work. Their chair designs were sturdy but genteel Sheraton fancy chairs, characterizing the mix of style appreciated by the Mormon pioneers and referred to as Mormon style. That design approach was known as *Country Sheraton* and exemplified the neoclassical style enjoyed by the fashionable of urban America and England.

Brigham Young purchased Sheraton chairs built by John and Thomas Cottam for at least three of his residences. There is little doubt that Young's enthusiasm for their style made them even more popular with Mormon Church members. (figure 2.31)

Sixty-year-old John Cottam and his wife Catherine arrived in the Great Salt Lake Valley with their sons in 1852. John had enjoyed a career as a woodcraftsman in England, as he descended from a long line of skilled tradesmen in that industry. His sons were similarly trained.

John Jr. settled in the Sixteenth Ward of Salt Lake City, building a home and turning shop on Fifth West and North Temple. The adobe-style shop was two stories high, with a large conical shed in the rear to house the machinery, which was run by hand at first and horse-drawn for operation later. Lumber was brought from the nearby mountains, while the iron parts were made in the blacksmith shop of Henry Cumberland on the opposite corner.

When the machinery was run by hand power, a man would turn a wheel that set the mill in motion; then the turner, John Cottam Jr., used various sizes of chisels to produce a piece of turned wood.

Horse-drawn machinery that was operated through a series of cogwheels greatly increased the production capability of the Cottam shop. In the ceiling of the shop, huge wooden cogwheels were secured. There was a vertical shaft in the center and a horizontal shaft fastened to it. At the end of the horizontal shaft, a horse was harnessed into position. A boy sat in a seat on the shaft to drive the machinery.

From 1860 until 1890, a variety of furniture and other wooden parts were fashioned in this manner. Chairs, tables,

FIGURE 2.31

SHERATON CHAIR
Thomas Cottam
Made for Brigham Young's farm
Elements of ladder-back and rod-back style, turned and spooled
Painted and grained, painted trim, rush seat
32 x 18 in.
Seat height: 16 in.
Collection of Pioneer Trail State Park

chests of drawers, bedsteads, potato mashers, and rolling pins were among the most common, while balusters, columns, and rosettes were made for the Salt Lake Temple, Tabernacle, Beehive House and Lion House. The chairs were typical Cottam designs in the Sheraton pattern with rush-bottom seats. John Cottam Jr. also made the furniture used in the first plays in the Salt Lake Theatre.

Though John Cottam Jr. established himself in Salt Lake City and his brother Thomas was called by the church to St. George in Washington County, both men made English-style, Sheraton-design chairs. These chairs usually had shaped stiles and ladder backs, the slats being separated by three turned spacers in the Sheraton manner. At least three types of these spacers have been documented as belonging to this Mormon pioneer period. The interesting distinction these chairs have is the adaption of English regional design to the different woods and rushes that existed in the desert of Utah.

Thomas Cottam, his wife, and five children had settled in St. George in 1862. We note in this journal entry, "He got work under Benjamine F. Blake who was a chair maker. He set up his own lathe run by man power, a large wheel six or eight feet in diameter, being turned to turn the lathe. His boys did the turning while he [Thomas] worked the lathe."[10]

Thomas Cottam brought with him the knowledge and templates acquired from turners in Yorkshire, England. The legs of the Mormon chairs he built in Utah are turned with the regional Yorkshire turning shapes and proportions, but the way he hung the seat on the front legs is unique to him.

The Cottam brothers, John Jr. and Thomas, had lived in Meadowland, Yorkshire, before they emigrated with their parents to America. The East Anglia region of England is very near to Meadowland. Anglian chair makers incorporated their traditional styles into the new nineteenth-century fashion of the Sheraton ladder-style chair back. All three Cottam furniture makers made chairs with ball spacers, and adopted the ladder-back chair's distinctive back to create their new "Mormon fashionable design." The nineteenth-century fashionable style of both of those regions was incorporated into the basic structure of the Cottam chairs.

Another element that gave these chairs an English character was the rush seats the Cottam men taught their wives to make, creating a complete family business. Once in Utah, Thomas found rushes on the Virgin River and John scouted for his rushes along the Jordan River farther north. Weaving rush seats was an arduous craft. The dry rush had to be wet for pliability in the twisting process where uniformity was prized and breakage was a constant challenge. Each seat took about three hours of tightly twisting the rush

to create the thin strands that fit tightly and symmetrically over the seat frame. It was a highly skilled occupation to achieve a seat of fine quality.

Master craftsmen, such as these and others to be discussed in this book, created a style of refinement in approximately twenty years that defined Salt Lake City and the cultural direction for the Mormon people. Their outstanding individual and collective contributions established culture that can be identified as Mormon high style.

The fact that they were willing to assist in the settlement and refinement of other towns in the colonization effort, while making furniture for "country" Mormons, clarifies how all communities were given equal priority and challenge in building Zion, the Kingdom of God.

FIGURE 2.32

COUNTRY SHERATON ROCKER
John and Thomas Cottam
Armless rocker with unique
    spool-pattern back
Pine
36 x 15 in.
Seat height: 15 in.
Collection of Pioneer Trail State Park

NOTES

1. Brigham Young, Letter to George Hickox, 19 February 1876, Ontario County Historical Society, New York.

2. Brigham Young, *Journal.*

3. Richard F. Palmer and Carl D. Butler, *Brigham Young: The New York Years* (Charles Redd Center for Western Studies, 1982), 11–16, Provo.

4. Brigham Young discourse of 20 April 1856, 3:323, chapters 1–4.

5. W. J. Mortimer, *How Beautiful Upon the Mountains* (Daughters of the Utah Pioneers) 27, 106, 272.

6. Joseph Openshaw, *Journal*, Daughters of the Utah Pioneers, Salt Lake City.

7. *Deseret News*, 16 August 1863.

8. *Deseret News*, As reported in Ralph Ramsay Journal, Richfield Centennial Home, Utah and National Historical registers.

9. Clara Ramsay Kotter, Daughters of the Utah Pioneers, records 367–69.

10. Thomas Cottam, *Journal* owned by family of great-granddaughters, Mrs. Nellie B. Gubler, and Mrs. Annie Jennings.

A Vision for Excellence

Based on their skill, individuality, and dedication, Mormon furniture craftsmen were called by the church to assist in the establishment of each community. As explained in previous chapters, most craftsmen who emigrated to Utah worked for a while in the Public Works projects in Great Salt Lake City.

Public Works

Public Works was begun in January of 1850. The first shops in that program to get underway were those of carpentry, blacksmith, machine, and painting. The placement of these shops close to the church tithing office indicates the organizational planning for every aspect of establishing the Mormon people in their new society.

Latter-day Saints contributed 10 percent of their increase to the church from its inception. When cash was a scarce commodity, goods or sometimes labor was contributed. The tithing contribution was, and continues to be, used primarily for welfare of those in need, who were expected to give service for receiving goods.

THE IMPORTANCE OF SCRIP TO CRAFTSMEN

In pioneer times, workers were hired by the church to work off their debt to the Perpetual Emigration Fund. They were paid in scrip which was redeemable at tithing warehouses for all the necessities of life. The craftsmen, particularly cabinetmakers and carpenters, and their families drew upon that resource, but in few cases was it their total income. This church resource was basic to the everyday life of the pioneer Mormon communities.

FIGURE 3.1
WARDROBE
Henry Dinwoodey, signed
Walnut front, poplar and pine sides, cottonwood case
Hinges from gun barrels of U.S. soldiers living in Camp Floyd
91 x 19 x 52 in.
Collection of Pioneer Trail State Park

How long a person worked for Public Works was determined by the amount of debt incurred to the Perpetual Emigration Fund that had financed bringing them to their new home. The craftsmen were needed to colonize other parts of the territory, so time spent in paying back the Perpetual Emigration Fund through the Public Works shops was minimal. Those converts who came without debt were immediately assimilated into the public sector.

Furniture was in great demand, and the furniture makers were busy. The finest cabinetmakers were given as many commissions as they could produce. The decision to manufacture the fashionable *Empire gondola chair* created a classic form that resulted in pieces as beautifully crafted as those from anywhere in the world. It is surprising that such quality was found in an introductory shop, testifying to the professional skill level of the craftsmen who brought their career experience with them. The Empire gondola chairs and the other furniture produced in these shops were labeled by a brand reading "Public Works/G.S.L.C.," sometimes including the date of manufacture. (figures 1.4, 2.9)

DESIGN FOR THE IDEAL SOCIETY OF DESERET

Since the Mormon colonization plan was to supply each community with professional people to build the towns, good design was part of the planning for the laying out of landscapes, thoroughfares, structures of all types, and architectural and interior design considerations. All aspects of commerce, as well as private and church life, were incorporated to create the ideal Deseret civilization.

Brigham Young had a great interest in establishing good taste in design throughout the territory. Many of the finest cabinetmakers eventually were sent to begin workshops for teaching journeyman skills to other converts, while supplying the people with functional and well-designed furniture, staircases, mantelpieces, and domestic implements. Private endeavor was always encouraged, but in the beginning most settlements needed the cooperative church organization for support before the individual workshops became self-sufficient. Almost without exception, every major community had an identifiable cabinetmaker.

Descendants of these furniture builders, today living throughout the nation, have kept an amazing number of pieces in their various family households. Small relic halls and museums that have preserved Mormon pioneer furniture also abound. Because these people also continue to respect the role their ancestral craftsmen played in the colonization effort, histories and journals have been preserved and made available as well. These communities and their key craftsmen are the focus of this chapter.

REGIONAL CRAFTSMEN DEVELOPED UNIQUE FURNITURE STYLES INFLUENCED BY THEIR DIVERSE CULTURAL BACKGROUNDS

Salt Lake County

Great Salt Lake City, located in Salt Lake County, was central to the establishment of all aspects of the Mormon culture. The first emigration and adjustment to the wilderness territory occurred there. The need for church conferences and private and commercial direction required a mobility to and from the city by the members of the leadership group. As colonization continued, the first and subsequent generations of Utah Mormons were linked to Salt Lake City for supplies as well as for cultural and spiritual activities.

Permanent settlement began in 1847 with the arrival of the first Mormon wagon train. Within the next few years, a dozen towns—dependent upon carpenters, cabinetmakers, joiners, and turners—were founded in the valley. Schools and musical and theatrical organizations also began during the first years, all calling upon the ingenuity of woodworkers to furnish items for their various needs. The craftsmen who could work with green as well as dried and cured wood were in demand. The Census of 1850 lists fifty-one woodcrafters of various skills. The number of American craftsmen led those from England, Ireland, Scotland, Wales, and Scandinavia by a slight margin.

FIGURE 3.2

WINDSOR CHAIR
John Cottam Sr.
Pine, grained, faux oak
Made for Salt Lake Theatre
27 x 21 in.
Seat height: 17 in.
Collection of Jonathan Sweet

FIGURE 3.3

BLANKET CHEST
Anonymous maker
Pine, grained
Rectilinear design
Made in Salt Lake County
18 x 33 x 17 in.
Collection of Richard Blanck

FIGURE 3.4

MANTELPIECE
Anonymous maker
Found behind remodeled wall in home
    built in 1865
Pine, grained
48 x 56 in.
Collection of Jonathan Sweet

By the Census of 1860, many of the craftsmen's names changed to simpler forms. Many other names dropped from the roster of Salt Lake County because those craftsmen had gone to assist in colonizing other areas. Listed in order of greatest population in Utah were emigrants from England, Wales, Scotland, the English Isles, and Ireland. The last of the heavy British emigration was in 1868. At that time, British-born emigrants made up 24 percent of the population. When their American-born children were added, these families made up as much as half of the population. Scandinavian emigration began slowly in 1852, with the heaviest emigration of Danish, Swedish, Norwegian, and Icelandic converts in 1862 and 1863. Most Scandinavians settled in Cache, Box Elder, Sanpete, and Sevier Counties. Quite a few changed their occupations from cabinetmakers, woodcarvers, turners, and joiners to carpenters, as the needs of each community were different in the steps of their settlement progression.

As the American-born craftsmen led in building the homes and other community buildings, the British led in establishing the taste of the furniture commissioned or bartered for other survival or material needs. By 1860, the Americans skilled in woodworking crafts numbered only half as many as the British and Europeans. The furniture-making industry became more competitive as the eastern furniture factories shipped hardwood furniture into the territory. The English and Europeans dominated the workshops that remained successful, despite the imported furniture in competition with their own.

Many of the cabinetmakers were able to find work through the entrepreneurs of the city, and others worked in their individual shops. Several of the most outstanding were given commission work by Brigham Young, and on occasion, he worked personally with a select few. Among those he worked with personally were Jesse Carter Little and Henry Dinwoodey, in addition to William Bell, Ralph Ramsay, and the Cottam men discussed in chapter two. It is interesting to become familiar with the craftsmen's particular role in the community, and varying amounts of information are available on those discussed here.

JESSE CARTER LITTLE

One of the original company of pioneers in 1847, Jesse Carter Little had helped arrange for the payment of the five hundred young men who made up the Mormon Battalion. Little's influence was also felt by Salt Lake City through his entrepreneurship of a manufacturing facility for wagons, carriages, and sleighs, as well as furniture. He also filled the roles of city cemetery sexton and marshal of Salt Lake City and was the first chief of the volunteer fire department.

At the Deseret Agricultural and Manufacturing Fair (D. A. & M. Fair) in 1860, Little was awarded $3 for the best bureau and a like amount for the best sofa. For placing second in the six-chair-set category, he received a diploma.

In 1862, he appealed for one wood turner and two cabinetmakers for bedsteads and tables, and by spring of that year he had entered into a partnership with Misters Hunt and Zitting. The *Deseret News* carried his advertisement in January 1862:

> *For the purpose of manufacturing extensively at J. C. Little's machine and work shops, in the 13th ward, every variety of furniture and cabinetwork including bureaus, secretaries, chests, wardrobes, tables and washstands, dressing tables, light stands, writing desks, bedsteads, sofas, single and double lounges, cradles, cribs, Boston and common rocking chairs, Windsor and common flag-seat chairs, children's small high and rocking chairs, French and flag-seat parlor chairs, etc.*

The same ad advised that the new firm would also manufacture doors, window sashes and blinds, spinning wheels, reels, swifts, flax-spinning wheels, hay rakes, grain cradles, etc., and could "if required, manufacture pianos, having the materials on hand for the purpose and competent workmen to attend to that department."

Pianos and other musical instruments would also be repaired. In exchange, Little, Hunt, and Zitting would accept cash, store orders [of supplies for people], grain, flour, beans, beef, pork, lard, eggs, butter, molasses, cheese, wood, cloth, wool, cotton, livestock, and "all kinds of valley produce which can be disposed of to enable us to carry on our business successfully."[1]

ERICK CAST

Cast was a cabinetmaker by trade whose following notice appeared in the *Deseret News* on 7 March 1860:

> *CABINET WAREHOUSE. I wish to inform my friends and the public generally that I have secured myself to the services of Mr. Powell, an experienced TURNER, and I always have on hand a variety of CABINETWARE—TABLES, BEDSTEADS, CHAIRS, &c., which will be sold at reasonable prices for grain, lumber, and provisions of all kinds. E. M. Cast, Half Block North of Emigration Street on State Road.*[2]

WILLIAM SMITH

An 1863 ad in the *Deseret News* of joiner and cabinetmaker William Smith, an emigrant from Ohio, read:

> *CHAIRMAKING IN THE 11TH WARD. W. Smith has on hand Windsor, Rush-bottom, Rocking, Sewing and other chairs of the best workmanship. Call and see me and bring your Lumber, Produce, Home-made cloth, etc. My shop will be found one block north of the Twelfth Ward School House. Wanted—5,000 feet 2 inch Cottonwood, Quaking Asp and White Pine.*[3]

FIGURE 3.5

Detail, wardrobe (figure 3.6)
Henry Pearson

GEORGE PARRAT

An item headed "Fine Workmanship" appeared in the *Deseret News* on 7 October 1868. It noted that a desk made by George Parrat from England, for A. W. Street, and constructed of walnut, common white pine, and two kinds of cedar was "equal in artistic design and beautiful finish to any that would be turned out in a first-class New York establishment. All its parts harmonize and the polish and beauty which it displays show the skill and hand of a master workman."[4]

HENRY PEARSON

Though little is known of him, Pearson had a workshop in Draper, Utah, in 1860, and some of his furniture pieces have been documented by the Salt Lake County Daughters of the Utah Pioneers (DUP). Note the ingenious detail of the built-in wooden hangers. (figures 3.5, 3.6)

FIGURE 3.6

WARDROBE
Henry Pearson, made in 1865
Pine, grained, faux oak
Built-in hangers most unusual feature
79 x 16 x 52 in.
Collection of Pioneer Trail State Park

HENRY DINWOODEY

An Englishman, born in Latchford of Cheshire, England, Dinwoodey wrote in his autobiography: "I did not receive the benefits of much scholastic education as at the early age of nine years, I commenced my career in life by obtaining work in a rope walk, my duties being to turn a wheel."

His father died when he was thirteen, and of that event he added:

> *I now felt it incumbent upon me to help mother all I could and was desirous of learning the trade of carpentry. I commenced an apprentice to Mr. Pierpont of Warrington, a builder by trade. I got along very well indeed for three years, at which time my employer died, that event canceling my engagement to him.*[5]

In 1845, Dinwoodey and his wife joined the Mormon Church, and three years later they and his brother emigrated to America, landing in New Orleans. There he obtained work immediately as a carpenter, making the equivalent of $12 instead of the three shillings a day that he had made in his native country. In April of 1850, he and his wife opened a notions and dry goods business in St. Louis, Missouri, but by 1853, the entire family prepared to move to Utah.

Arriving in Salt Lake City by wagon in mid-September 1855, he recorded in his journal, "I hired space in other wagons to bring in dry goods and other articles that I wished to bring into the country." Since trading and bartering were common means of exchange in the valley at that time, Dinwoodey became very successful. That same year, he went into the carpentry and cabinetmaking business with James Bird, and they located their shop on East Temple (now Main Street).

By the spring of 1858, according to Dinwoodey's autobiography, orders were received from the leadership that due to the impending invasion by the U.S. Army, all inhabitants should vacate the city and the northern Mormon settlements, and move south. A committee remained behind to set fire to all the houses and lay the whole country waste as soon as they received word from church leaders.

Dinwoodey wrote later:

> *After our arrival in American Fork Canyon, myself and partner went to work and repaired an old saw mill and commenced to manufacture shoe pegs and make lumber and thus passed our time until towards the end of the summer.*

Dinwoodey joined the Mormon Militia, and since the war between the U.S. government and the Mormon Militia was averted by negotiation, the U.S. Army was allowed to camp south of Salt Lake City. Their needs were a new source of economic livelihood for the Mormons. Henry Dinwoodey made use of their need for supplies by trading goods for goods. Army rifle-metal was used to make such furniture parts as hinges on wardrobes. (figure 3.1)

The wood available in American Fork Canyon, fifty miles from Salt Lake City, appealed to Dinwoodey. He advertised for wood in the *Deseret News* in 1862:

WANTED at H. Dinwoodey's Furniture Warehouse, opposite the Telegraph Office, 26,000 feet of Lumber as follows: 8,000 ft. of 2 in. White Pine, Cottonwood [sic] or Quaking Asp Plank, 7,000 ft. of 1 in. White Pine; 2,000 ft. 1½ in. of Red Pine. Also, about 30 or 40 cords of Red Pine or Quaking Asp Wood, for which I will exchange Furniture of all kinds, spinning wheels, etc.[6]

Dinwoodey later wrote in his journal:

The only mode I had of paying my men being to exchange and barter furniture for the curious products of the country, such as lumber, adobes, beef, home made boots and shoes; provisions etc. was always done for a trade, scarcely came amiss, even to beet molasses and soft soap, there was no regular pay day but whenever a man required anything I gave him an order on certain tradesmen with whom I kept a credit account or note and paying the amount by exchange of my goods.

By the use or mode of barter and exchange, I enabled many of my employees to obtain lots, and homes of their own. When any one of them stated to me he wished to purchase a certain lot and build himself a home, I would trade for the land for him and give him an order on the lumberman, adobe maker, brickmason etc. and by this means he would get his house built and repay me by his labor. When which payment was completed I would give him a deed for his property.

FIGURE 3.7

DINWOODEY SHOP
Cabinet and chair shop
Collection of Utah State Historical Society

By September of 1864, Dinwoodey announced in the *Deseret News:*

EXTENSIVE CABINET ESTABLISHMENT! H. Dinwoodey having made important additions to my shops, and having on hand a Large Quantity of Seasoned Lumber for the Manufacture of every description of CABINETWARE, and being now engaged in further enlarging my work-shops and warerooms, I take pleasure in announcing to my friends and the public that I am prepared to fill orders to any amount in the line of Household Furniture. I shall, in a few weeks, have a complete stock of Undertaker's trimmings from the States which will enable me to furnish COFFINS on short notice and in the best Style of workmanship. SHOPS: on East Temple St. Opposite the Telegraph Office and on First South Street west of the Meat Market. WANTED: about 30,000 feet lumber 4 x 4 Scatling 12, 14, 16 feet long; White Pine 3 x 4 [inch].[7] (figure 3.7)

FIGURE 3.8

HENRY DINWOODEY
Dinwoodey, standing in his shop after
   railroad was completed in 1869
Note imported Thonet rocker, bent wood
Photo: collection of Utah State Historical
   Society

FIGURE 3.9

TABLE
Henry Dinwoodey
Pine, painted and grained, faux bird's-eye
   maple
Simple and elegant Empire design
41 x 27½ in.
Collection of Pioneer Trail State Park

Dinwoodey was always looking for the newest tools and machinery to facilitate a large manufactory of furniture. In 1866, he purchased a new ten-horsepower engine, enabling him to turn his lathe, drill, and circular saw. Aware that the first transcontinental railway was close to completion, he traveled to the East Coast and ordered furniture and machinery that included a planer, and mortising and shaping machines to expand his production capabilities.

By 1867, his inventory of furniture was extensive. His diary from this period tells of his business acumen leading to directorships of numerous businesses, as well as his city appointments to director of Zion's Cooperative Mercantile Institute (ZCMI), the first department-style store west of the Mississippi; director of Deseret National Bank; regent of the Deseret University; and chair of a committee to investigate the subject of homemade glue.

Dinwoodey was a practicing polygamist with three wives and nine children. When polygamy was made illegal, he was sent to prison for six months because he refused to send two of his wives away. His first wife died while he was in jail, though he was permitted to visit her once during her illness and to attend her funeral. His furniture-making business continued with his partners and employees in his absence.

Dinwoodey later summarized his business success, in spite of his personal challenges, in his diary:

> *I have now a still increasing business requiring still more store room in order to carry it on, which commenced in 1857, with a few home-made tables and chairs, amidst all the difficulties arising from a young country situated over a thousand miles from a railroad in any town of commercial importance, has gradually grown with the city and its surroundings to be the largest furniture business between Omaha and California, commenced on the stock worth but a few dollars but which gradually increasing in quantity, variety, and price now in 1887 over One Hundred Thousand Dollars in value.*[8] (figure 3.10)

Many of the finest craftsmen in the territory worked with Dinwoodey, either as employees or as part of an association. The diary of Edmund Fuller Bird related his experience with Dinwoodey:

> *While working at my trade, on June 18, 1868 the Cabinet Makers of the city met at Dinwoodey's Furniture Factory pursuant to appointment to take measures for organizing into a society for manufacturing purposes. H. Dinwoodey was called to the chair and Edward Hanham, Esq. was appointed secretary. William Bell, R. Ramsay, W. L. H. Allen, Edmund F. Bird, Thomas Higgs, James Bird, and Capener were appointed to draft rules for the Society and report tomorrow. So the Dinwoodey Furniture Store came to be.*[9]

FIGURE 3.10

DINWOODEY BLOCK
Dinwoodey's furniture store built in 1890
Furniture was shipped all over western
 states
Collection of Utah State Historical Society

Most of these members of the association were from England, where they had gone through the steps from apprentice to master. As exceptional craftsmen, they were important in establishing English taste and furniture techniques in Salt Lake City.

WILLIAM L. N. ALLEN

William L. N. Allen was one of the finest cabinetmakers in the state. He emigrated from England, where he had lived in Kingston-upon-Hull in the county of York. His diary explains his furniture training there: "Between the age of fourteen and fifteen, I was bound as an apprentice to William Barry of Hull to learn cabinet making, with whom I served seven years or so."

By contrast to what Allen experienced after his emigration to America much later on, he experienced the harsh working conditions of an apprentice in England during the 1840s. Like others, he worked from six in the morning until seven in the evening. Along with one hundred other appren-

FIGURE 3.11

TOOL

William L. N. Allen's furniture-making tool
Collection of Stephen Shepherd

FIGURE 3.12

TILT-TOP OCTAGON
PEDESTAL TABLE
William L. N. Allen
Inlay on table top made from hardwood-
   box parts
26½ x 32 in.
Collection of Barbara B. Nielson

tices, he joined a grievance committee that was able to change working conditions to a limited degree, by boycotting the workplaces for a short period. He and many of the others spent some time in jail before their efforts met with any success. The success amounted to being given time to have their "Tea, which we had not had before," Allen recorded in his journal.[10]

William Allen and his wife Hannah joined the Mormon Church in October of 1848. By 1851, he was appointed to be president of the Hull England Branch. He baptized his childhood friend William Brown, a shop carpenter who went yearly to the Arctic seas to fish for whales. Brown convinced the Allens to emigrate to America and assisted them in doing so.

For seven years, William Allen was a carpenter for the Public Works church shop in Great Salt Lake City, to square his debt with the Perpetual Emigration Fund. He progressed from living in a tent to building his own home within a year of his arrival. He and his sons carried on the business of contracting and building in the community.

Allen built several of the Fort Douglas buildings for the U.S. Army. At the same time, his cabinet shop did a considerable business in furniture and turning. Allen's association with the Dinwoodey group of fine cabinetmakers is verified by the journal entry of Edmund Bird. The impact of the imported goods affected him as it did the other wood artisans, and his profession became more carpenter than cabinetmaker.

On 20 December 1887, the *Deseret News* described the stature that Allen's furniture work had achieved: "On display at the John C. Cutler store was a beautiful inlaid table, the work of Bishop W. L. N. Allen, one of the finest craftsmen in the country."[11] (figures 3.11, 3.12, 3.13)

FIGURE 3.13
Detail, octagon pedestal table (figure 3.12)
William L. N. Allen
Inlay pattern made from hardwood-box
   parts

EDMUND FULLER BIRD

Bird came from London, England, from a wood trade, immigrated to Canada, and then moved his family to Boston, Massachusetts, in 1842. They were affiliated with the Mormon Church. His first wife died in 1845, and he married Cordelia More Martin of Vermont in 1847. By 1850, he prepared to immigrate to Utah, arriving later in that same year. He recounted in his journal:

> *I lived on Third South just north of Pioneer Park. I raised twelve children and kept busy making furniture for many homes in the area and doing what I could to help build up the Kingdom. I also did much of the carving on the decoration inside the Tabernacle, especially on the organ.* (figures 3.14, 3.15)

FIGURE 3.14

DRESSER
Edmund Fuller Bird, made in 1870
Imported mahogany, pine, and
cottonwood
Victorian design, hand-carved
85 x 23 x 46 in.
Collection of great-grandson Ted Bird

Detail, dresser (figure 3.14)
Edmund Fuller Bird

His assignment was to work with Ralph Ramsay, considered to be the finest wood carver in the entire Mormon culture. They worked together on the Tabernacle organ. He was requested to join the fine cabinetmakers in the Dinwoodey group. Both of these honors speak highly of his superb craftsmanship and resourcefulness with available materials and tools. He won awards at the D. A. & M. Fair in 1861 for best center table and best bedstead.

In 1862, he was called to go as a missionary to England, returning to Utah in 1865. In 1867, his wife Cordelia died, leaving nine children. He married Lucy Boll of London and Elizabeth Steadman of Sweden. Diversity of people and traditions is most apparent in this family where the cultures of England, Ireland, New England, and Sweden mingled. Bird supported his large family, thus: "I worked at my trade, and made many pieces of beautiful furniture that the brethren bought for their homes."[12]

JAMES BIRD

James Bird is listed as a joiner from England in early references, and later as a carpenter in 1860. He was a partner of Henry Dinwoodey from about 1856 to 1858. Together they moved their families to American Fork Canyon when the Saints were instructed to flee before Johnston's Army. He and Dinwoodey explored the canyon and discovered large stands of pine. He settled in Provo and from there was called to the Cotton Mission in St. George.

THOMAS HIGGS

In 1860 and 1870, the census shows Higgs as a carpenter from England. His name appears in the household accounts of Brigham Young as one who was

STAIRCASE
Beehive House woodwork was done by
William Bell, Ralph Ramsay, and
  Thomas Higgs
Architectural elements of Beehive House,
  LDS Church

personally selected to help build and furnish the Beehive House. His participation in the Dinwoodey Association indicated his furniture business commitment for the entire city, not just for his patron. Even though no furniture has been located with an identifying Higgs mark, his craftsmanship is evident in the structural components of that home. (figure 3.16)

REGIONAL CABINETMAKERS, TURNERS, AND CHAIRMAKERS ESTABLISHED MORMON MATERIAL CULTURE

A discussion of cabinetmakers and turners is best organized according to the counties where they carried on their craft, because all stages of settlement were going on at the same time. Some towns in a region were building and furnishing prominent homes, while members of others were still living in forts. Though cabinetmakers and carpenters were sent to begin and develop settlements, some communities were close enough to established towns that the cabinetmakers could supply furniture for a region rather than a single community.

Central Utah, Utah, and Tooele Counties

FIGURE 3.17

ROD-BACK CHAIRS
Left rocker: David Cluff
Pine, painted
26 x 14½ in.
Seat height: 15½ in.
Collection of great-great-granddaughter
  Mrs. Elizabeth Conover Reynolds

Right chair: David Cluff
Pine, painted
28 x 15 in.
Seat height: 15 in.
Collection of great-great-granddaughter
  Beverly B. Hansen

Utah County was settled in 1849. Its earliest settlers lived in a fort until they made a peaceful coexistence with the Indian people. Homes were generally equipped by family carpenters. But by 1852, some of the Provo people were advertising their manufactured products, such as David Cluff and his son H. H. Cluff, along with R. R. Rogers, who notified the public through the *Deseret News* that they had "opened a cabinet shop; [with] good furniture made from well-seasoned Box Elder."

DAVID CLUFF JR., UTAH COUNTY

Born in June of 1795 in Nottingham, Rockingham County, New Hampshire, David Cluff joined the Mormon Church in 1832. He helped construct the church temples in Kirtland, Ohio, and Nauvoo, Illinois. The family arrived in Salt Lake City in October of 1850, and then moved to colonize Provo in Utah County. An 1868 newspaper notice read: "Provo Cabinet Shop! David Cluff Jr. Proprietor. Furniture constantly on hand. Cheap to cash or produce." An upholstered, scrolled Empire settee was illustrated with the announcement.

Later, he and his son W. W. Cluff were sent to colonize Wasatch Valley. When he was eighty, he went to teach and establish furniture workshops in Gila Valley, Arizona. He was one of many craftsmen sent to set up workshops and teach fine craftsmanship in difficult-to-settle communities.[13]

FIGURE 3.18

SUGAR BIN AND CHAIR
Bin: anonymous maker
Pine, grained, faux bird's-eye maple
23 x 13 x 20 in.

Chair: Walter Huish
Pine
32 x 14½ in.
Seat height: 15 in.
Both, Collection of John Told

SEELEY OWEN, UTAH COUNTY

An American from Milton, Vermont, Owen was born in March of 1805. While living in Nauvoo, Illinois, he worked on the temple. In 1847, he arrived in Utah with the first party and was assigned to Provo in 1849. There he built a cabinet and turning-lathe shop, equipping it with a waterwheel for the manufacture of furniture of all kinds. He made the first bedstead, chairs, baby cribs, spinning wheels, clock reels, and other pieces of household furniture used by his family and many Provo residents. In 1870, he was sent to Wallsburg, Utah, and later to Arizona.[14] (figure 2.1)

WALTER HUISH, UTAH COUNTY

Huish had brought his family to Great Salt Lake City in 1849 and then returned to St. Louis in the spring of 1851 to bring his patterns, shafting, pulleys, and cutter heads across the plains by ox team. With Warren Tenney, a machinist, he operated a machine shop that combined cabinetry with carpentry.

In 1853, Huish was sent by Brigham Young to Payson in Utah County to begin one of the first furniture factories in Utah. Prior to settling in Payson, he had made patterns of a planing machine and an engine lathe while employed in St. Louis. Establishing a planing mill and furniture factory on

the corner of Second South and First East Streets was the fulfillment of his business goal. The business was so successful that he was able to give work to more tradesman than any other furniture enterprise of his time.

In 1862, Huish was joined in business by James Finlayson, listed as a cabinetmaker from Scotland, with whom Huish had worked in St. Louis. His knowledge as a millwright was unique, and together they framed and furnished a planing mill.

The Huish firm manufactured spinning wheels, tables, chairs, bureaus, bedsteads, cabinets and wardrobes, as well as coffins. The W. H. Huish and Sons Furniture Company supplied most of the settlements in Utah County with sturdy and practical furniture made from local softwood.[14] (figures 3.18, 3.19, 3.20, 3.21)

WILLIAM CHRISTIANSEN, UTAH COUNTY

Christiansen was one of the many woodcraftsmen who, by 1868, had settled in Pleasant Grove in Utah County. He came from Denmark, where he had been a carriage maker. As there was little call for carriages in the Utah Territory, he went to work for the Dinwoodey Furniture Company to learn the trade. He later moved to Provo, joining Harvey and David Cluff's shop to learn cabinetmaking. He also became a caregiver and an herbalist, and was therefore highly relied upon in his community.

His small Pleasant Grove shop provided a facility for his creative use of

FIGURE 3.20

CHEESE SAFE
Made by Isaac Losser in 1863
Swiss design influence
71½ x 36½ x 41 in.
Collection of Welsford H. "Gus" Clark

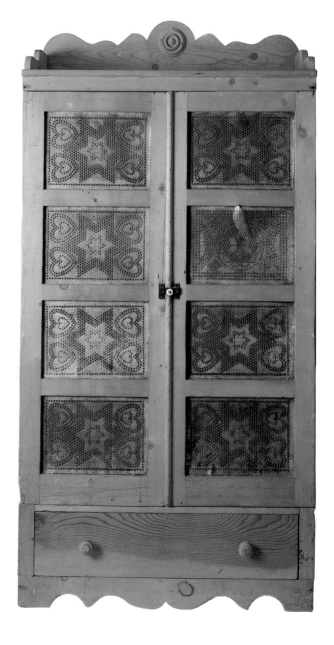

FIGURE 3.21

FOOD SAFE
Attributed to Isaac Losser
Note star of David detail
71½ x 36½ x 41 in.
Collection of LDS Church, at Lagoon
   Corporation

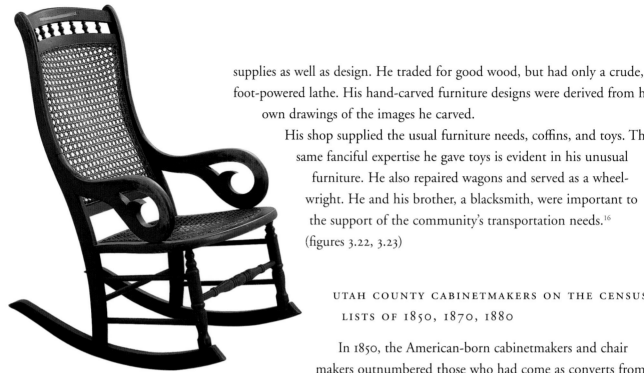

supplies as well as design. He traded for good wood, but had only a crude, foot-powered lathe. His hand-carved furniture designs were derived from his own drawings of the images he carved.

His shop supplied the usual furniture needs, coffins, and toys. The same fanciful expertise he gave toys is evident in his unusual furniture. He also repaired wagons and served as a wheelwright. He and his brother, a blacksmith, were important to the support of the community's transportation needs.[16] (figures 3.22, 3.23)

FIGURE 3.22

ROCKING CHAIR
Made by William Christiansen in 1872
Pine, painted and grained
Hand-scrolled arm, cane back and seat
41 x 19 in.
Collection of Pleasant Grove DUP

UTAH COUNTY CABINETMAKERS ON THE CENSUS LISTS OF 1850, 1870, 1880

In 1850, the American-born cabinetmakers and chair makers outnumbered those who had come as converts from foreign shores.

ENOS CURTIS, chair maker from New York

WALTER HUISH, furniture maker from England

LEIR W. HANCOCK, cabinetmaker from Massachusetts

JAMES McCALL, cabinetmaker from South Carolina

DAVID CLUFF JR., cabinetmaker from New Hampshire

SEELEY OWEN, cabinetmaker from Vermont

ISAAC LOSSER, furniture maker from Switzerland

In 1870, the changes in population were indicated by the census, as was the impact of imported East Coast goods. Of the 14 cabinetmakers listed, the breakdown of their place of origin was as follows: America, six; Britain, five; France, one; Sweden, one; Switzerland, one. By 1870, all but Walter Huish and Isaac Losser from the 1850 Census had moved on to help colonize other areas. (figures 3.20, 3.21)

In the 1880s, the impact of imported goods changed the opportunities for cabinetmakers. Emigration from England and the Scandinavian countries, where fine cabinetmakers were still receiving craftsmanship training, is apparent in this census.

The population of Utah County had grown significantly by 1880, but only twelve cabinetmakers were listed on the census: six from Britain, two from America, two from Denmark, one from Sweden, one from Switzerland.[17]

Tooele County

One of the original six counties in Utah formed in 1850, Tooele County is located in the western basin-and-range country; it has mineral-rich mountains and the Great Salt Lake Desert. Early sawmills and gristmills were built, but little cabinetmaking was carried on. Sheep and cattle herds and mines rich in silver, lead, and zinc were the sources of wealth in Tooele County. Mormon ranchers also developed large sheep and cattle herds that ranged over the vast desert. All of these settlers could afford to trade for their furniture needs with Salt Lake County makers.

The total number of thirty-three carpenters and two cabinetmakers listed for thirty years' worth of Tooele census figures makes us assume that Salt Lake City supplied Tooele County's needs. The two cabinetmakers listed are William Dunn from Scotland, and David Burnett. Burnett advertised in the *Deseret News* in July of 1864: "Wanted: A wood turner to run a turning lathe and circular saw, propelled by water power—One who has knowledge of fitting up furniture would be preferred."

WILLIAM DUNN, cabinetmaker from Scotland
DAVID BURNETT, cabinetmaker [origin unknown]

FIGURE 3.23

SINGLE LOUNGE
William Christiansen
Pine, grained, faux mahogany
Unique carved back rail, unusual arm
    upholstery, removable
42 x 26 x 81 in.
Collection of Pleasant Grove DUP

FIGURE 3.24

CHILD'S WINDSOR ROCKER
John Powell
Pine, painted
27 x 15 in.
Seat height: 12 in.
Collection of State House Museum
 in Fillmore

FIGURE 3.25

TOOLS
Furniture-making tools belonging to
 John Powell
Collection of State House Museum
 in Fillmore

South Central Region of Juab, Millard, and Beaver Counties

In 1851, the Salt Creek community, later renamed Nephi, was settled. By 1852, the legislature created Juab County, a narrow strip on the western boundary of the Utah Territory, which today is the western boundary of Nevada. The western portion of this original county was reduced in 1854 and 1856 when Nevada gained the area. For the more than twenty years during which local carpenters built structural necessities, the residents acquired their furniture from neighboring counties, probably Utah and Sanpete.

By the 1870s, Nephi as county seat became a thriving livestock and railroad distribution center. Imported furniture was available to the area. Few cabinetmakers were listed in the census. There was strong interdependence between the towns in Sanpete and Juab Counties, though the Juab people were predominantly Scandinavian and Sanpete people were English. The cabinetmakers from Juab included the following:

A. M. JENSON, cabinetmaker from Denmark

ERICK PETERSON, turner from Sweden

T. G. SCHRODER, cabinetmaker from Denmark

THOMAS RICHARD SCHRODER, apprentice cabinetmaker, Utah

Millard County began in 1851 with thirty families selected by the church to establish the town of Fillmore. It served as the capital of the Utah Territory from 1851 to 1856, and then continued as the county seat. The community's importance to the organization and management of Utah required Fillmore to have buildings of prominence and substance early in its development. Thirty carpenters were active from the 1850s to the 1880s, but only three cabinetmakers were listed.

JOHN POWELL, cabinetmaker from England
MORTON MORTONSON, cabinetmaker from Denmark
WILLIAM STEWART, cabinetmaker from England

JOHN POWELL

An Englishman from London, Powell came to Utah in 1856. He moved his family to Meadow, a small village close to Fillmore, in 1868. Having been a carpenter in England, he came equipped with a hammer, saw, and turning lathe.

FIGURE 3.26

SECRETARY/BOOKCASE/DESK

John Powell

Pine, grained, faux walnut and bird's-eye
    maple

Turned legs, unusual bonnet

82 x 31 x 38 in.

Gift of Don Carlos Young Estate,
    Collection of Pioneer Trail State Park

Though he taught school for a short time, he soon changed his occupation
to furniture making. His wife Henrietta moved all the household articles to
one end of their single-room home so that the remaining space could serve
as his furniture shop. Later, he and William Stewart formed a partnership
and built a frame lean-to at the side of his house to be used for a carpentry
shop. They made cradles and beds "of distinction" and beautiful chairs
called *Congress chairs* for adults and children. They made "interesting" desks
and tables. Their workshop was the major local supplier of furniture for the
region.[18] (figures 3.24, 3.25, 3.26)

WILLIAM STEWART

William Stewart's emigration from England to settle in Utah is classic for Mormon pioneers. On arrival, he provided a dugout plus a covered wagon for a bedroom, where his family stayed while he hauled timber from the hills and constructed a log room. He made all the useful articles of furniture and later built a two-story home. D.U.P. records show that he was a cabinetmaker and that he also built and decorated all the caskets in his county, charging a minimal sum.

Central Eastern Counties of Sanpete, Sevier, Emery, and Grand

FIGURE 3.27

BED
Anonymous maker
Owned and possibly made by
  Lindsay Anderson Brady
Pine, grained
56 x 59 in.
Fairview, Sanpete County Museum

Many towns in the central eastern counties weren't established until the 1880s, and they struggled as settlements far longer than most Utah communities which were self-sustaining. Though the Indian tribes of Utah and the Mormon Church leaders worked for cooperation with each other, Indian problems caused some settlements to be abandoned. Perhaps twenty years later, another attempt at colonization occurred. Aridity, grasshoppers, harsh heat, and severe cold all made colonization extremely difficult.

In the 1850s, Sanpete County was settled predominantly by Americans. Kentuckian Lindsay Anderson Brady, a carpenter, helped settle Nauvoo, Illinois, before immigrating to Utah and Fairview in Sanpete County.[19] (figure 3.27)

The 1850 Census shows no Scandinavian carpenters nor cabinetmakers but does show that 90 percent of such craftsmen were American. James Watkins was the lone Englishman; Charles Blanfees, the only German, was a chair maker; and Samuel Gifford was a chair maker from New York.

Of the fifteen carpenters and cabinetmakers listed in 1860, seven are Americans, three are English, one Swedish, one Swiss, and three Danish. The cabinetmakers listed then are listed here:

FIGURE 3.28

TABLE DESK
Anonymous maker
Desk used for signing of the Black Hawk
    peace agreement of 1861
Pine, grained
59 x 33 in.
Collection of Mt. Pleasant Relic Hall

FREDRICK COLLENS, cabinetmaker from England

THOMAS JACKSON, cabinetmaker from England

ANDREW MILLICK, cabinetmaker from Massachusetts

Along with the change in the population of these counties, the numbers of furniture craftsmen and their countries of origin changed as well. In the 1870s and 1880s, more Scandinavians arrived. By the 1870 Census, twenty-seven carpenters and cabinetmakers from the Scandinavian countries worked with five Englishmen and seven Americans in the same trades.

Sanpete County went through these population changes partly because it was impacted by the Ute Indian uprising that resulted in the Black Hawk War. The desk used for the 1861 signing of the Black Hawk peace agreement can be seen in this chapter. (figure 3.28)

The 1880 Census lists thirty-seven in the woodcrafting trades from Scandinavia, eight from England, one from Canada, and ten American-born.

NIELS CHRISTENSEN, cabinetmaker from Denmark

NIELS JENSEN, cabinetmaker from Denmark

I. H. LARSEN, cabinetmaker from Sweden

HANS MAGLEBY, cabinetmaker from Denmark

ANDREW MORTENSEN, cabinetmaker from Sweden

PETER A. MORTENSEN, cabinetmaker from Denmark

OTTO OLSEN, cabinetmaker from Norway

PETER PAULSEN, cabinetmaker from Norway

PETER PETTERSEN, cabinetmaker from Sweden

ANDERS SWENSEN, cabinetmaker from Norway

The visual taste of these two decades of craftsmen—and their customers—gave a unique Scandinavian design to the overall Mormon furniture style of the pioneer period. A more comprehensive report of the Scandinavian furniture makers and their great contribution to beauty and function in furnishings will be discussed in chapter four. Two cabinetmakers' stories, however, need to be included here.

HANS O. MAGLEBY OF SEVIER COUNTY

Hans Magleby, having come from Dragor, Denmark, had completed his apprenticeship in 1856. By 1859, he was in Utah, where he quickly found work as a cabinetmaker. He worked for some time with the Dinwoodey Furniture Company and later had a furniture shop in Salt Lake City. In

FIGURE 3.29

CUPBOARD
Anonymous Scandinavian maker
Pine, original grained finish has been
 stripped
95 x 44 x 41 in.
Collection of LDS Church

FIGURE 3.30

BOOKCASE
Anonymous Scandinavian maker
Made for Manti Temple
Pine, painted and grained
83 x 42 x 34 in.
Collection of John Told

CUPBOARD
Anders Swenson
Pine, painted and grained
79 x 43 x 41 in.
Collection of Dale Peel

November of 1864, he reported in his autobiography, "I sold my shop to Mr. Stever for $1,200. Bought another cow for $60 and hay for $56 a ton and a plow for $90." The comparative value of the furniture shop to the other items indicates the Mormon society's great regard for cabinetry.

In 1875, the call came to move to Sevier County, where the United Order was in force. The hope for establishing a city of fine craftsmanship is apparent because the top cabinetmaker and carver in Utah, Ralph Ramsay, was a director in the order. Magleby settled in Monroe and established a mercantile institution, a furniture workshop, and a store. He accumulated lands and herds and built comfortable homes for his families. He accepted two missions to the Scandinavian countries and traveled to donate his skill in constructing and furnishing the temple in Manti, Utah.[20]

ANDERS SWENSEN OF SANPETE COUNTY

Anders Swensen settled in Mt. Pleasant in Sanpete County after having immigrated from Oslo, Norway, in 1865 to the Salt Lake Valley. His daughter, Sarah Swensen Madsen, wrote in the family history:

Father worked at his trade as a carpenter and cabinetmaker making tables, chairs, cupboards and all kinds of home-made furniture. He built quite a nice home in Mt. Pleasant, and he worked as a carpenter in Salt Lake City on the Salt Lake Theatre and the Jennings building.

Swensen was called by Brigham Young to donate his time as a carpenter in helping with the fine work of the St. George Temple. He was paid in groceries and clothing from the stores, and in scrip for the rest. He was away for several years working for the Manti Temple, which was completed in 1888.[21] (figure 3.31)

Southern Utah Territory

Iron County was settled in 1851 with the first town of Parowan. From there, groups were sent to settle other communities, including Cedar City, Paragonah, New Harmony, Kanarraville, Panguitch, Snowflake in Arizona, and Las Vegas in Nevada.

Experienced craftsmen arrived and trained others to supply the needs of the new communities. Many of the most experienced cabinetmakers, joiners, and millers were of the original company to enter Parowan. Their

FIGURE 3.32

WINDSOR CONGRESS CHAIR
Thomas Durham in the PUMMI shop
Made for the Durham family home
27 x 25 in.
Seat height: 17 in.
Needlepoint seat added later
Collection of Mrs. Barbara Durham Hatch

FIGURE 3.33

DOUBLE LOUNGE
Attributed to Thomas Durham
Empire scroll elements
Pine, grained
40 x 27 x 82 in.
Parowan United Manufacturing Institute

furniture was produced in areas often more arid than their counterparts in the Great Salt Lake area of Utah.[22]

Elijah Elmer established the first cabinet shop in the area. Ebenezer Hanks, who had been with the Mormon Battalion that found gold in California, took up freighting on the southern route between Los Angeles and Salt Lake City. After settling in Parawan, he shared ownership in a mercantile business and built a tannery, a cabinet shop, and a cotton factory. When pine was needed for the Tabernacle organ pipes, he located the required lengths of wood and transported them three hundred miles by ox team to Salt Lake City.

Francis T. Whitney made a good grade of cut nails and cast handsome brass door handles, latches, and other small metal articles used on furniture.

Thomas Durham arrived in 1856 as a Martin Hand Cart Company veteran, having been a wood-turning expert for a cotton-thread factory in Manchester, England. His skill as a wood turner resulted in fine chair spindles, bedposts, stair rails, etc., when he immigrated to Utah. He also built coffins and added his skills as composer, choir director, and speaker at funerals and other church services.[23]

Eventually the cabinetmakers of the town organized a company and store called the Parowan United Manufacturing and Mercantile Institution,

FIGURE 3.34

FOUR-DRAWER TABLE
PUMMI maker, 1880
Pine, oak veneer
36 x 21 x 30 in.
Top hinges and lifts up
Collection of Parowan DUP, Old Rock
    Church

which was known as P.U.M.M.I. or P.U.M.I. By 1877, it was a flourishing business, and its furniture was used throughout the southern region. Thomas Durham and James Connell operated the furniture-manufacturing business. (figures 3.32, 3.33)

The 1860 Census recorded five carpenters in the Beaver County area, but by 1870, there were seven carpenters and two cabinetmakers. The 1880 Census lists thirty-eight carpenters and two cabinetmakers. Though the area was remote and deprived of many of the enriching cultural activities of urban communities, residents such as Swiss emigrant H. E. De Saules, a tradesman in Kingston, Beaver County, used the mail service as a lifeline. His diary discusses how he spent all of his extra money sending for tools, templates, books, and eastern and European newspapers.[24]

FIGURE 3.35

PRESIDENT'S CHAIR
Anonymous maker
Made for the St. George Temple
Black willow, bent wood, painted white
36 x 22 in.
Seat height: 17 in.
Collection of St. George DUP

FIGURE 3.36

CHAIRS
Thomas Cottam and Benjamin F. Blake
Made for the Jacob Hamblin home
Pine, with rush seats
41 x 17 in.
Seat height: 15 in.
Collection of LDS Church,
  Jacob Hamblin Home

Washington and Kane Counties

Brigham Young sent small groups into southwestern Utah as early as 1852 in a colonization effort to establish an overland route to the Pacific Ocean and Southern California. Six settlements were begun. Colonization was less of an experiment after 1861, when several hundred families were called to raise cotton, figs, olives, grapes, sugar, and almonds. The boundaries of Washington County stretched the entire width of the territory, about six hundred miles at that period. The present size and shape of that county were reconfigured in 1892.

Brigham Young had a home built in St. George in Washington County. The town's important stature in this hot-climate area resulted from church leaders coming to meet with President Young on church and territory administration concerns, from the cultural offerings that were organized there, and from the agricultural industries possible in a climate with less severe winters: cotton, wine, and molasses. The climate and the genteel lifestyle garnered southern Utah the nickname of "Dixie."

Homes were built of thick adobe in an effort to provide cooler interiors in the extreme heat of the harsh desert climate. Also known as the Cotton Mission area, St. George and surrounding communities received the calling assignments of many colonists whom Young selected for their outstanding leadership in establishing communities in other arid environments. George A. Smith, after whom St. George was named, John Menzies MacFarlane, and Indian interpreter Jacob Hamblin were among those key men appointed to the area.

Brigham Young's enjoyment of the sturdy, pine Cottam-family chairs purchased for his Salt Lake Valley homes influenced him to request Thomas Cottam to produce the same elegant chairs for the residents of St. George. (figures 3.35, 3.36)

Thomas Cottam and Benjamin Blake established workshops in St. George that supplied furniture to local settlers and, in 1877, chairs to the St. George Temple. Blake used wood or rawhide for chair bottoms, in contrast to Cottam's rush-bottom chairs.

Cottam worked as a turner and chair maker in much the same way as he had done while serving his apprenticeship in England. Because his specialty was rush-bottom chairs, he found the rushes from the marshlands along the

FIGURE 3.37

DIXIE ROCKER
Anonymous maker
Pine, painted
39 x 21 in.
Seat height: 15 in.
Collection of LDS Church,
  Jacob Hamblin Home

Virgin River particularly useful to his business. His chairs were characteristically made in the *Sheraton fancy* manner and were quite similar to the chairs his father and brother produced in Salt Lake City.[25]

Census reports for 1860, 1870, and 1880 list woodcrafters of importance to the Dixie area:

BENJAMIN F. BLAKE, chair maker and upholsterer from England

WILLIS COPLAN, carpenter, cabinetmaker, and turner from Virginia

THOMAS COTTAM, chair maker from England

SAMUEL K. GIFFORD, chair maker

JAMES EARL, cabinetmaker from Ohio

WARREN HARDY, wood turner from Massachusetts

JOHN N. HINTON, cabinetmaker from England

JOHN H. CARLING, cabinetmaker of importance from the United Order of Orderville, Kane County. (Chapter four discusses Orderville United Order cooperatives.)

Davis County

Recognizing the agricultural potential of the Davis County area, early pioneers moved livestock into the area for winter forage. By 1850, a number of small settlements were active, and by the 1870s, this area was the garden spot of Utah. The material culture of the area was developed by the predominantly English- and American-born craftsmen who settled there. Bountiful and Centerville were two communities where cabinetmakers established workshops. For several, documentation exists for the particular wood furnishings they produced in individual shops:

JOHN J. HARRIS, craftsman from England, had a shop in Centerville, where he made Congress chairs and wooden utensils.

JOHN PERRY, cabinetmaker and wheelwright from America, had a shop in Bountiful, where he made tables, chairs, chests of drawers, cupboards, wagons, and carts.

WARRINER PORTER, craftsman from America, made bedsteads laced with rawhide strips.

THOMAS WHITTAKER, cabinetmaker, carpenter, scenery designer, and silkworm grower, was awarded $2 first prize for the best lady's workbox at the D. A. & M. Fair of October 1861.

FIGURE 3.38

EMPIRE BED
Anonymous maker
Pine, grained, faux crotch mahogany
Headboard: 54 x 54 in.
Footboard: 48 x 54 in.
Collection of Dr. & Mrs. E. Ute Knowlton

FIGURE 3.39

BOSTON ROCKER
Made in William Capener workshop,
    member of Dinwoodey group
Pine, stained
42 x 25 in.
Seat height: 17 in.
Collection of Lagoon Corporation

WILLIAM CAPENER, carpenter and cabinetmaker from England, drafted
    the rules for the Dinwoodey Furniture Association.
SOREN JACOBSEN, carpenter from Denmark, made railings used in the
    Bountiful Tabernacle and coffins for the settlers.

Census figures list twenty-two English carpenters and ten American carpenters who were the dominant designers of homes and furniture in Davis
County.

Weber County

A crossroad area at the spine of the Wasatch Mountains, with valleys extending to the Ogden and Weber Rivers, Weber County appealed to trappers
and Indians, as well as pioneers. Permanent settlement began in 1843, when
horse trader Miles Goodyear built a fort and trading post on the bank of the
Weber River. Goodyear sold his claim to James Brown, a veteran of the
Mormon Battalion, who paid $1,950 in gold coins.

By 1850, the Ogden settlement had grown to over eleven hundred residents, making the transition from fort to individual homes by 1858. Minerva
Stone Shaw described the home built there by her blacksmith father in her
diary:

FIGURE 3.39a

LADDER-BACK CHAIR
Anonymous maker
   owned by Amos Pease Stone
Pine, rush seat
36 x 14½ in.
Seat height: 14 in.
Collection of Ogden DUP

The first house father built in Ogden in 1858 was of pine logs, on the corner of Twentieth Street and Washington Boulevard. It had two rooms, one on the ground and an upstairs bedroom. Mother's bedstead was a bird's-eye maple, made in Salt Lake City by a Mr. Miller. The chairs were the old fashioned rush bottom chairs. We had one rocking chair brought from Connecticut, a tall clock, a stepstove that father riveted on some wagon tires stretched across the wagon box while crossing the plains. There were three panes of window glass 8 x 10 inches side by side on one side of the house. We had a fireplace, a comb case, a wall pocket, a pin cushion hanging on the wall, a looking glass and a knifebox, all brought from the east. (figure 3.39a)

The importing of goods such as those in the Stone family was a typical practice on the wagon-train and handcart immigrations of the period.[26] (figure 2.3)

After the railroad to Ogden was completed in 1869, the town became a supply center, and imported goods were plentiful. Few cabinetmakers are recorded in Weber County between 1850 and 1880. Because there were few of them, their local importance was magnified:

PETER A. BOYLE, cabinetmaker and carpenter from Scotland, made tables, chairs, beds, bookcases, chests, and cupboards. After the railroad completion, he established a successful furniture store.

ENOCH BURNS, cabinetmaker from Canada

WILLIAM McGARY, cabinetmaker from Canada

ALFRED CARISWELL, wood turner from England

FRANCIS P. JENSON, cabinetmaker from Denmark

DANIELE WILSON MURDOCK, chair maker from Indiana

JONATHAN BROWNING, pedestal parlor-table maker and rifle maker, owned Ogden's first powered lathe. He later became one of the greatest producers of rifles in the United States and the world.

The census figures between 1850 and 1880 recorded the carpenters by immigrant or American origin: fifty-six Americans, fifty-eight British, ten Canadians, twelve Scandinavians, and five Dutch.

Northeastern Utah, Morgan, Summit, and Wasatch Counties

Though settled in 1855, Morgan County was not created until 1862. Its residents played a critical role in supplying Mormon soldiers and harassing Johnston's army during the Utah War. The mountainous area had been attractive to fur trappers and to several Indian tribes during the fur-trading days of 1820–40. Since this county has some of the finest pine forests in the Wasatch area, it became important in 1860 for supplying lumber to construct buildings, furniture, tools, and implements of all kinds.

The 1870 Census recorded Morgan County's craftsmen:

OLE STODDARD, cabinetmaker and carpenter from Illinois

HANS MAGLEBY, cabinetmaker from Denmark. Magleby was typical of fine craftsmen sent to assist in the colonization of new areas. He settled in Salt Lake, Morgan, and Sevier Counties.

Summit County was created from the combination of Green River and Salt Lake Counties in 1854. The Uintah Mountains dominate the eastern portion of the county; the Wasatch Mountains formed a high-backed valley to the west, and both were great sources of lumber, coal, silver, lead, and zinc.

FIGURE 3.40

FOUR-POSTER BED
Anonymous maker
Light graining, painted black decorative
    outline
Owned by apostle Amasa Lyman
48 x 47 x 58 in.
Collection of John Told

Park City was founded in 1872, and its rich silver and gold mining supplied great wealth within and outside Utah.

Carpenters, assigned to Summit County by the church between 1860 and 1880, included twelve British, twelve Americans, three Scandinavians, one Swiss, two Prussians, and one Canadian. There were no cabinetmakers listed, providing the accepted assumption that imported goods—including furniture—were purchased by all economic levels of citizens from Salt Lake City, Heber, or Midway.

Wasatch County attracted German and Swiss settlers because of its Heber Valley area. The climate is classified as highland, offering cool summers and severely cold winters. The moisture is helped by both snow melt and numerous rivers. Wasatch County is called "Little Switzerland" because the mountains are high and dramatic and the residents from Switzerland recreated their homeland's distinctive architecture.

The carpenters and cabinetmakers recorded included: seven from America, three from England, and two from Switzerland.

WILLIAM BELL, cabinetmaker from England

In 1866, William Bell, one of the finest craftsmen in all of Utah, was called on a mission to set up a cabinet shop in Heber. His calling included the training of others in the art of fine cabinetry. He made furniture in the Wasatch County area until three years before his death in 1886. (figures 2.9–.17)

W. W. CLUFF, and his father DAVID CLUFF JR.
> set up a lathe and cabinet shop in Coalville. They made chairs for the new settlements.

J. ROBEY, cabinetmaker from Illinois, made cupboards, tables, and
> bedsteads in Midway, after having learned the trades as a worker on the Nauvoo Temple.

MORONI BLOOD, cabinetmaker from Illinois, made and repaired many
> types of furniture and cabinets and made caskets.

Unique in Utah history is the settlement of Duchesne County. In 1861, President Abraham Lincoln created the permanent home of the Uintah and White River Utes. Later the Uncompahgre Utes were moved to the Uintah Mountains. This county's settlement did not occur under the direction of the Mormon Church colonization effort. It was settled by individuals who obtained 160 acres under the Federal Homestead Act. They paid $1.25 per acre, and after five years of living on the land and making improvements, the homesteaders were given title to their property.

The 1880 Census records list:

JOSEPH BLACK, cabinetmaker from Pennsylvania
PATRICK CARROL, carpenter from New Brunswick

Northern Utah, Cache, Box Elder, Rich Counties, and Southern Idaho

Cache County began with the settlement of Maughan's Fort by Peter Maughan in 1856. (The name has been changed to Wellsville.) By 1859, five towns had been settled: Providence, Mendon, Logan, Richmond, and Smithfield. The towns were begun and organized by craftsmen called to colonize the area. Franklin was settled later than these.

FIGURE 3.41

LADDER-BACK CHAIR
Made for John Bair, a large man requiring
  a large and sturdy chair
Pine, painted
45 x 24 x 22½ in.
Seat height: 17 in.
Collection of Richmond DUP, Relic Hall

FIGURE 3.42

PEDESTAL TABLE
Cornelius Travelier
Cedar, unusual clear finish
Sixteen-sided top, turned base
30 x 43 (diameter) in.
Collection of Richmond DUP

The 1860 Census included:

CHARLES GRAY, chair maker from England

CHARLES OLSEN, cabinetmaker from Norway (figure 3.43)

By the 1880 Census, both the population and the need for craftsmen in wood may be assumed from the records of Cache County's communities:

Hyrum: eight carpenters, of whom four were Scandinavian, three American, and one Prussian.

Wellsville: eight carpenters, of whom six were British, two American, and one,

DAVID STODDARD, was a cabinetmaker from Scotland.

Millville: two carpenters, one from Denmark and one from England.

Providence: two carpenters, of whom one was Swiss and one English, and three cabinetmakers:

CHARLES YOST, from Switzerland

JASPER THORNTON, from Canada

HENRY HAFTER, from Switzerland

Logan: fourteen carpenters, of whom eight were Scandinavian, three British, two Canadian, and one Russian, and cabinetmakers:

NICHOLS JACOBS, from Switzerland

CHRISTIAN OALASEN, from Denmark

NEILS PETERSON, from Denmark

NICHOLAS ZOMER, from Switzerland

Smithfield: two carpenters and two cabinetmakers:

PRESTON MOREHEAD, from Mississippi

JAMES A. JACKSON, from England

Hyde Park: two carpenters:

JOYN EYNCE, from Scotland

JAMES HANCEY, from England

Richmond: four carpenters, one being from Missouri, two from England, and one from Norway.

Franklin: three carpenters, one being from Kentucky, one from Scotland, and one from Vermont.

Oxford: one carpenter from Scotland and one cabinetmaker,

RUEBEN BURFEE, from Canada

Mendon: one carpenter from England[27]

Logan: seventy-five carpenters were listed in its 1880 Census: thirty-five Scandinavian, thirty-five American, twenty English, ten Prussian, six Swiss, and four from Baden. Though carpenters were plentiful, only six cabinetmakers and turners were recorded in all of Cache Valley. A large amount of lumber was being produced, but little of it was being used for furniture following the advent of the railroad.

The Logan cabinetmakers and turners were:

HANS J. HANSEN, turner from Denmark

NIELS L. A. LINDQUIST, cabinetmaker from Sweden.

FIGURE 3.45

LOUNGE
Dr. James Hancey
Empire design elements
40 x 27 x 79 in.
Extension: 27 in.
Collection of Sharon Meikle

Lindquist emigrated to Cache County in 1868. His furniture was considered fine enough that families have passed it down for generations. His Scandinavian designs were different from the Scandinavian pieces in Sanpete County. (figure 4.17)

Other woodcraftsmen in the county were:

CHARLES OLSEN, cabinetmaker from Norway

FREDERICK W. HURST, cabinetmaker from Utah

WILLIAM A. CALEB, cabinetmaker from Baden

PRESTON T. MOREHEAD, cabinetmaker from Mississippi

DR. JAMES HANCEY, dentist, inventor, carpenter, cabinetmaker from England. He built chairs, cupboards, tables, beds, cradles, washing machines, and toys. Caskets built in his shop were lined with cloth and padded with cotton batting.[28] (figure 3.45)

Bear River Valley

EDWARD McGREGOR PATTERSON

Patterson emigrated to Utah from Northumberland, England, in 1858. At that time, the area was part of Utah, but by 1871, it had become part of Idaho. Carpenters and cabinetmakers moved back and forth across the border and joined efforts to build the tabernacle in Paris, Idaho and the Logan Temple. McGregor supplied furniture for the area from his shop in Bloomington, Idaho, and built homes as well. His wives wove the carpets for the Logan Temple. (figure 3.46)

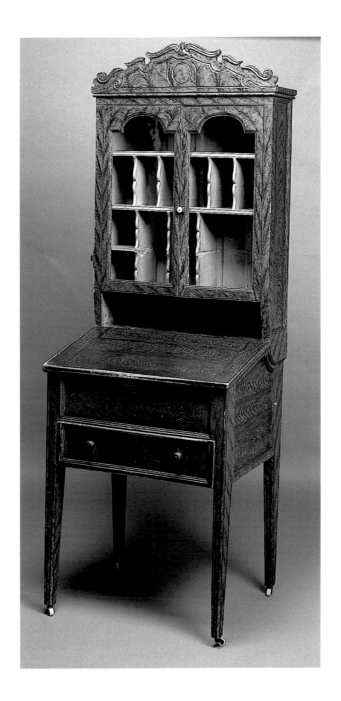

FIGURE 3.46

DESK
Edward McGregor Patterson
Pine, grained
90 x 31½ x 26 in.
Hutch: 11 in. deep
Collection of LDS Church

Box Elder County

MATHEW DALTON

Dalton was the earliest cabinetmaker in Weber County. He moved to
Willard in Box Elder County to establish an important cabinet shop. Dalton
is discussed in chapter one.[29] (figure 1.17)

Brigham City information is included in chapter four, but several
important craftsmen who made furniture before the Brigham City Cooperative Mercantile and Manufacturing Company was formed are listed here
with their county:

FIGURE 3.47

MATHEW DALTON WORKSHOP
Perry, Box Elder County

JUDGE SAMUEL SMITH, cabinetmaker

MR. WALKER, cabinetmaker from the East Coast

The origin of the following craftsmen is unknown:

ASMUS JORGENSEN

OLE POULSEN

WILLIAM WRIGHTON

The census entries between 1850 and 1877 show twenty-nine carpenters and cabinetmakers. Outstanding among them were:

ORSON PULSIPHER

J. DEDRICKSON

MARTIN LUTHER ENSIGN[30]

FIGURE 3.48

PLANING MILL
Merrill Planing Mill, built in 1863
Produced planed lumber and furniture
    parts, Brigham City

This chapter paints a broad picture of the vision for a genteel Christian society that Mormon pioneers held while colonizing the western wilderness. Their progression from dugout shelters and cabins within fortified walls to two-story log or adobe homes and elegant mansions was due to the capabilities and vision held by individual craftsmen in each community. The excellence of work by expert craftsmen was not limited to urban centers. The church called craftsmen of similar expertise to each settlement to provide buildings and furniture of comparable quality. The next section will explore the artisans' diversity of skills and taste that produced what has become known as Mormon furniture—an eclectic blend of the finest craftsmanship and the most popular styles of the regions of the world from where the craftsmen immigrated, brought to bear upon the limited wood resources of Deseret.

FIGURE 3.49

FOUR-POSTER BED
Made in Brigham City, anonymous maker
Unique thistle design as finials on posts
Headboard: 56 x 52 in.
Footboard: 50 x 52 in.
Collection of Brigham City Corporation
Museum

NOTES

1. *Deseret News*, January 1862.
2. *Deseret News*, 7 March 1860.
3. *Deseret News*, advertisement, 1863.
4. *Deseret News*, 7 October 1868.
5. Henry Dinwoodey, *Journal* and history owned by the family of Henry and James Dinwoodey, Salt Lake City.
6. *Deseret News*, 11 June 1862.
7. *Deseret News*, 7 September 1864.
8. See note 5 above.
9. Edmund Fuller Bird, *Journal* owned by great-grandson, Ted L. Bird, American Fork.
10. W. L. N. Allen, *Journal* and history owned by great-granddaughter, Barbara B. Nielson.
11. *Deseret News*, 20 December 1887.
12. See note 9 above.
13. David Cluff Jr., *Journal* owned by great-great-granddaughter, Beverly B. Hansen.
14. Seeley Owen, *History* owned by great-granddaughter, Elizabeth C. Reynolds, Salt Lake City.
15. M. C. Dixon, *Peteetneet Town, a History of Payson, Utah*.
16. Daughters of the Utah Pioneers, *Builders of Early Millard County*, 368–9.
17. See note 16 above.
18. See note 16 above.
19. Lindsay Anderson Brady, *Journal* and history owned by great-great-grandson, Rodney Brady, Salt Lake City.
20. Hans O. Magleby, *Journal* owned by the Hans O. Magleby Foundation.
21. Anders Swensen, *History* and letter to family in Norway owned by grandson, Frank Swensen, Mt. Pleasant.
22. L. A. Dalton, *History of Iron County Mission*.
23. Thomas Durham, *Journal*.
24. H. E. De Saules, Utah State Archives.
25. Thomas Cottam, *Journal* and history owned by great-granddaughters, Nellie B. Gubler, and Annie Jennings, St. George.
26. Daughters of the Utah Pioneers, *Minerva Stone Shaw, Stories from our Museum*, Weber County.
27. Utah Census 1870, 1880.
28. *Utah Journal*, 2 December 1885.
29. *History of Dr. James Hancey*, owned by the family of James Hancey and Doris Reeder.
30. Daughters of the Utah Pioneers, *History of Box Elder County*, 1937, 118–22.

Exceptional Furniture Through Diversity and Cooperatives

❊   ❊   ❊

The nineteenth century was a period of social, economic, and cultural change throughout the world. The converts to The Church of Jesus Christ of Latter-day Saints left their home countries and traditions for a new way of life in a difficult desert. They took direction from a powerful leadership and, through organization, created a society that accepted their diverse languages and cultures. The Mormon Church valued individual talents; each member was important to the good of the whole.

Immigrant converts from foreign countries and from states within the Union were dynamic because the teachings of their Christian church gave them hope for a better life. They were willing to take great risks and make the necessary sacrifices to fulfill the church prophecy of a new temporal and spiritual society. Wherever they settled, their homes and furniture were practical while expressing a new style that mirrored the finer values of the cultures where they were brought up.

MANUFACTURED FURNITURE IMPORTED BY RAIL IMPACTED MORMON CRAFTSMEN IN UTAH

Research by Dr. Thomas Carter, an architectural historian, documented Sanpete County furniture styles. He addressed the composition, decoration, materials, and techniques of Sanpete craftsmen. His explanation is built on an internal logic which has created a valuable resource of documentation that historians can draw upon. Some key assumptions to the unique styles he categorized are as follows:

Symmetry in design was the key to the cupboards design. Within the formal constraints of the symmetrical model, however, great variation occurred, suggesting either that individual shops produced a large number of designs, or

FIGURE 4.1

CUPBOARD
Fredrich Christian Sorenson
Pine, painted and grained faux walnut
Original hardware, glass doors, spoon rack
84 x 21 x 41 in.
Collection of great-grandson Kenneth
  Sorenson

more likely, that many different cabinetmakers were producing cupboards in the same basic style. The most important structural option was a narrow row of drawers placed in either or both of the cases that added six to fourteen inches to the height of the cupboard. (figure 4.1)

All cupboard types were highly decorative. The standard embellishment had cresting at the top above a small and rather simple cornice. Most crests were doweled into the top board and were invariably symmetrical, divided into three parts, the larger middle element emphasizing the center point of the design and repeating the symmetry of the cupboard below. The base was often treated similarly, many pieces had a symmetrical scroll-cut apron. (figures 4.2, 4.3)

The preferred decorative details on the cupboards were split spindles. The spindles were formed by ripping a board in half and then gluing it back together. It was then turned on a lathe, either in a turn or a spool pattern and then re-split along the seam. The resulting halves were applied to opposite sides of the case, generally vertically to the outside rails. Round medallions were occasionally applied to the lower doors, crests, and aprons, but such devices were much more common on beds and lounges.[1] (figure 4.4)

FIGURE 4.2

CUPBOARD
Anonymous Danish maker
Pine, grained faux rosewood, inside painted
  blue
Turned and split detail
77 x 16 x 48 in.
Collection of Tom Carter

In some areas of Utah, the individual workshop was the place where furniture originality was manifested. But economic survival was jeopardized after 1875 when goods of all kinds flooded into Utah via the railroad. A common characteristic of wanting to be part of the dynamics of society manifested itself when the railroad brought goods to Utah that the pioneers had done without for many years. The flood of eastern goods caused havoc with the Mormon economy. The group's need to take care of its religious and economic viability forced the Mormons to alter their approach to the style of wood-crafted products and the strategy for manufacturing them. The resulting decline of cabinetmakers is very evident even in areas that are remote. However, United Order cooperatives in Utah competed with imported goods for a longer period than did smaller, independent shops.

Two successful approaches developed in different parts of Utah need to be addressed. The *Brigham City furniture style* was developed to meet the burgeoning markets of Victorian style. The *Orderville furniture designs* solved the needs of a simple, self-sustaining agricultural society. These

FIGURE 4.3

CUPBOARD
Anonymous Danish maker
Pine, painted, inside painted blue
78 x 17 x 45 in.
Collection of Mrs. Ann Carter

workshops could not have been successful if the diversity of the people working in them and the diversity of the buying public had been less compatible and acceptable. These two cooperative approaches, though two of many, were the most important and will be discussed in detail later in this chapter.

Perhaps the diversity of people who produced furniture that was practical in style as well as function can best be appreciated by studying the *double lounges* produced throughout Utah. Double lounges were popular in the West, Canada, Nova Scotia, Scandinavia, and even on passenger ships traversing the oceans. Those built in Utah were made of soft rather than hardwood which affected the design solutions created by Mormon craftsmen.

The lounges were shaped like a long rectangle to accommodate a reclining person lengthwise. They were generally formed by two frames with

alternating bed slats. One frame pulled out to make a double bed. The movable frame didn't have a back rail. The practicality of the double lounge made it a standard piece of furniture in most homes. Later, the style was altered to a single lounge which became equally popular. Backs were added in a variety of designs. (figures 4.5–.11)

FURNITURE FASHIONS WENT DIRECTLY TO UTAH FROM EUROPE, ENGLAND, SCANDINAVIA, AND EASTERN AMERICA

The Scandinavian people played a significant role in the furniture making of Utah. Coming from Denmark, Sweden, Norway, and Iceland, they brought the Nordic traditions into most communities to some degree. The largest group of these people were called to Sanpete and Cache Counties, where winters were as harsh as those of their native countries. Smaller populations settled in Box Elder and Sevier Counties. The land offered good agricultural possibilities, and both areas flourished in the raising of crops, sheep, turkeys, and cattle.

Communities varied in their proportion of people from a specific Scandinavian country. Multi-ethnic communities were the rule in all the territory, but some towns in both Sanpete and Cache Counties had a predominance of Scandinavian carpenters and cabinetmakers who worked for the Scandinavian residents. With so many different languages in each community, the family's first language was spoken in the home and English was adopted as the second language. Sometimes there were understandable language barriers to information exchange and commerce. However, an amazing assimilation occurred in most communities.

In both Sanpete and Cache Counties, cabinetmakers in the 1850s were predominately English and American. By the 1860s and 1870s however,

FIGURE 4.5

DOUBLE LOUNGE
Anonymous maker
Pine, grained faux butternut
Empire scroll elements
34 x 27 x 89 in.
Collection of LDS Church

FIGURE 4.6

SINGLE LOUNGE
Anonymous PUMMI maker
Pine, painted and grained faux
  crotch mahagony
38 x 25 x 79 in.
Collection of John Told

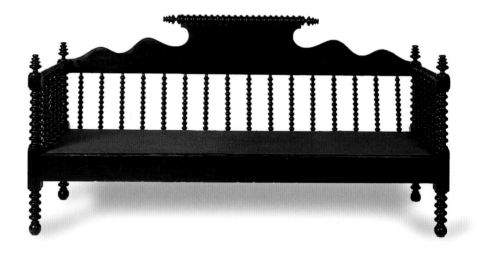

FIGURE 4.7

SINGLE LOUNGE
Anonymous maker
Pine, stained ebony
Unique spooled posts and finials
36 x 27 x 71 in.
Collection of LDS Church

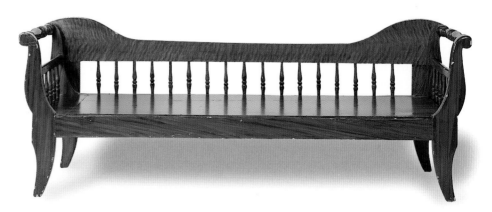

FIGURE 4.8

SINGLE LOUNGE
Anonymous maker
Pine, painted and grained faux mahogany
29 x 27 x 83 in.
Collection of LDS Church

FIGURE 4.9

DOUBLE LOUNGE
Anonymous maker
Pine, painted and grained faux ebony
38 x 86 x 27 in.
Collection of St. George DUP

FIGURE 4.10

EMPIRE SINGLE LOUNGE
Anonymous maker
Pine, unusual light graining, crotch pattern
32 x 24 x 77 in.
Jointly owned by the families of
    Mr. & Mrs. Willard Richard Lund and
    Mrs. Minerva Stone Shaw, Collection of
    Ogden DUP

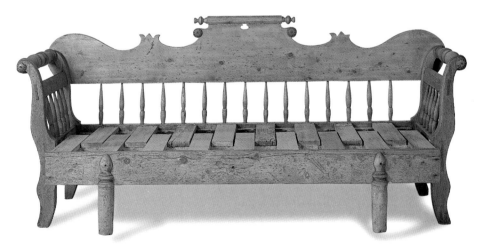

FIGURE 4.11

DOUBLE LOUNGE
Anonymous maker
Pine, has been stripped
Unusual additional legs support bed when
    extended to double width
31 x 27 x 71 in.
Collection of LDS Church

FIGURE 4.12

TABLE

Anonymous maker

Pine, painted and grained faux
   crotch mahagony

Table extension has holes for broom
   handles to support extra boards

Collection of John Told

carpenters and cabinetmakers reflected the population shift to more Scandinavians, Northern Europeans, and British.

The furniture made by these dedicated craftsmen was constructed within the traditions and shared aesthetic conventions of the finest designs in the countries they had left to emigrate.

The style of fashion in Europe, England, Scandinavia, and Eastern America is known by a variety of names, but it is Empire in the period between 1850 and 1870. This design style took its direction from the classical reproductions of furniture forms found on the ancient Greek vases lauded by Emperor Napoleon of France.

Simplicity and the use of exotic woods, such as rosewood, became the style rule in every country. Since design trends move with the craftsmen who develop them, it is important to keep in mind that the master craftsmen coming to Utah created designs in keeping with the newest fashion, not the old traditions.

Art historian Jules Prown contends that the unstated cultural principles and values of a society are "most clearly perceivable, not in what a society says it is doing in histories, literature, or public and private documents, but rather in the way it does things."[2]

The Mormon cabinetmakers supplied communities with furniture and home necessities and in so doing established design criteria based on their knowledge and expertise. They shared the dream of creating a better, new society and recognized their importance as craftsmen in its visual shaping. The environment was harsh, but the culture in these early settlements was genteel. Furniture makers also created rails and spindles for the carpenters who built staircases and occasionally crafted whole staircases themselves. They made moldings and window sashes for homes, public buildings, and Mormon meeting houses, tabernacles, and temples. (figure 4.12, 4.13)

The simple designs and sturdy construction of Scandinavian furniture appealed to the Mormon virtues of simplicity and practicality and were easily adapted to the woods found in the region. These factors explain the universal appeal of the *day couch* used for a single or double bed as well as for seating that was not particularly comfortable. It was a variation on the single and double couches popular at the time throughout Europe and the East Coast of America. The designs of these couches produced in the various Utah communities were unique from one another, but style in a region became dominant when patrons and cabinetmakers were of the same nationality.

The tradition in the Scandinavian countries of painted or grained

FIGURE 4.13

BOOKCASE DESK
Morton Rasmussen
Pine, grained
Entire piece: 84 x 38 in.
Desk: 29 x 38 in.
Collection of Ester Rasmussen Christiansen

FIGURE 4.14

ROCKER
Swalby Bjerregaard
Pine, painted
41 x 24 in.
Seat height: 17 in.
Collection of Mrs. Helen Rigby

furniture was an immediate success with the cultural attitudes of the rest of the Mormon Anglo-American membership. The vogue in the United States was to cover the less-than-fashionable woods with painting or graining. In Sanpete Valley, this called for painting the local pine to resemble exotic hardwoods such as mahogany and walnut. In the 1860s, a dark red mahogany was the favored wood to imitate, but by the 1870s the choice was dark walnut. By the 1880s oak was the preferred faux treatment.

POPULATION CONCENTRATION OF SCANDINAVIAN CRAFTSMEN CREATED REGIONAL STYLES

Between 1860 and 1880, the census shows over sixty-one cabinetmakers were working in Sanpete County. The mixture of the ethnic population showed forty-two were of Scandinavian origin: twenty-six Danes, three Norwegians, and eight Swedes. The largest group emigrating from England numbered seven, and the rest were emigrants from all over the United States. This dominance of Scandinavian furniture designers was the greatest in the territory.

At the same time, only twenty-six cabinetmakers were in the combined numbers of Cache, Box Elder, and Rich Counties of Utah, and those of southern Idaho settlements. Statistics show the Scandinavians, especially the Danish, to be in the majority: four Swiss, five Americans, three English, one Canadian, two Scots, eight Danes, one Swede, and two Norwegians. Comparison of the regions stylistically shows that outside the traditional furniture made in all the territory, there are few similarities in details.

Little is known of the actual shops. It appears that small operations were the rule, with a single cabinetmaker working alone, perhaps with a helper or apprentice. The workshops in Cache County and in Sevier County, where communities of Scandinavian cabinetmakers lived, were similar to those in Sanpete County, where towns were peopled predominately by Danish, Norwegian, and Swedish immigrants. Few craftsmen are singled out by name in historic records. The following were repeatedly mentioned, though specific details of their importance are limited to the information given here. (figure 4.14)

CARL UCKERMAN

Norwegian Carl Uckerman ran the largest private operation, a water-powered factory in Ephraim, employing four turners and joiners. Ephraim also had a church-sponsored cooperative furniture shop. According to a local newspaper correspondent, in 1869 it was "doing a good business, some specimens of work, especially several center tables, being elegant in design and finish."

ANDERS SWENSEN

Family records show Anders Swensen arrived in Utah in 1865 and was sent to Mt. Pleasant. There he worked at his trade as a carpenter making tables, chairs, and cupboards. He built a nice home which he wrote about to his relatives in Norway in 1877:

> *Some news we can bring you, we have recently exchanged our home and lot with our neighbor, and received a home and lot from him, and he will give us $400.00. He is going to be a merchant in our house, and we are going to build again because it is too little and poor a house. We are going to move in a few months, but we are first going to harvest each our places. We have 50 apple trees, pears, apricots, and plums of which 0 [zero] will bear fruit this year. The place where we are taking over there are only 14 fruit trees.*[3] *(figure 4.15)*

FIGURE 4.15

SINGLE LOUNGE
Anders Swensen
Pine, painted and grained faux walnut, stenciled
36½ x 26 x 79 in.
Collection of Mr. & Mrs. Dennis Tucker

Swensen worked on the Salt Lake Theater and the Jennings home in Salt Lake City. He was called to work without cash payment on the St. George Temple, and for several years on the Manti Temple. From 1872 to 1888, the Manti Temple was being built by labor that was paid in food and scrip negotiable in church stores. This payment was not unusual for outstanding craftsmen. It was considered a blessing to be called to do work on the holy buildings, as it is today. Excellence in craftsmanship was a criteria equal to devotion to the church in the selection of artisans for this vital church work.

HANS MAGLEBY

Hans Magleby of Sevier County also tells in his personal history of being called to work on the Manti Temple. Though he had to leave his home, he felt it worthwhile because he was able to "acquaint myself with the modern methods employed in cabinetmaking." He had been employed in cabinetmaking since he was apprenticed in Denmark in 1849. For more than thirty years, he had been making furniture and was pleased at the Manti opportunity to try new styles and new skills. He took pride in his accomplishment of being one of those responsible for the most famous staircases in the Utah Territory—the spiral staircases in the ends of the Manti Temple. After about six months of this labor mission, he returned to his family in Monroe, Sevier County, in March of 1885.[4] (figure 4.16)

NIELS LINDQUIST

Niels Lindquist learned his trade in Sweden in 1863 and emigrated to Cache County in 1868. His stylistic designs were quite different from the furniture produced in Sanpete County. Instead of painting or graining the pine, he finished his furniture in clear varnish. His unique furniture was considered fine enough that families have passed it down generation after generation. His personal solution to surviving the railroad bringing manufactured furniture to Utah was to expand his coffin business and adapt himself to becoming a full-service mortician.[5] (figure 4.17)

FIGURE 4.16
FOOD SAFE
Hans Magleby
Pine
61 x 42 x 41 in.
Collection of Dr. & Mrs. Nilson Ephraim

FIGURE 4.17

SINGLE LOUNGE

Niels Lindquist, 1860

Pine, flat vase spindles on back

Hinged top; blanket box base slides out

37 x 24 x 83 in.

Collection of Logan DUP

TRADITIONAL UTAH FURNITURE BECOMES LESS POPULAR, FORCING CRAFTSMEN TO MAKE A LIVING SOME OTHER WAY

After the railroad came in 1867, traditional furniture, whether imported from the converts' native countries or made in American regions, was not as popular in Utah as it had been earlier. Outstanding craftsmen had to find alternative ways to support themselves and their families.

By 1877, Anders Swensen's traditional furniture, for example, was not in demand by the fashion conscious even in his rural Mormon, predominantly Scandinavian town. Swensen wrote:

> *It is our intention to buy more land, because our children are growing up and*
> *they are going to help us work our place, and carpenter work is not too good*
> *in our city as it had been. Furniture is imported from the East and from*
> *California, and windows and doors together with moldings for homes are*
> *all brought in here, so it looks like I have to rely most on remaining a farmer,*
> *tilling the earth.*

COOPERATION, THE NECESSITY FOR GROWTH

Brigham Young strongly believed in social equality and opposed gradations of wealth and status among the people. He consistently encouraged the widest ownership of the new cooperatives to prevent the development of a wealthy privileged class. At the same time, he recognized that if the Mormons became integrated into a national economy they would become mere suppliers of raw materials. Then they would be forced to repurchase their own products in manufactured form at a comparative economic disadvantage.

In a sermon on 8 October 1868, Young summed up his opinion of the Mormon Churches' stand on trade:

> *How our friends, the outside merchants will complain because we are going to stop trading with them! We cannot help it. It is not our duty to do it. Our policy in this respect, hitherto, has been one of the most foolish in the world. Henceforth it must be to let this trade alone, and save our means for other purposes than to enrich outsiders. We must use it to spread the Gospel, to gather the poor, build temples, sustain our poor, build houses for ourselves, and convert this means to a better use than to give it to those who will use it against us. We have talked to the brethren and sisters a great deal with regard to sustaining ourselves and ceasing this outside trade. Now what say you, are you for it as well as we? Are we of one heart and one mind on this subject? We can get what we wish by sending to New York for it ourselves, as well as letting others send for us. We have skill and ability to trade for all we need; and if we have to, we will send our agents to buy and bring home what we need. My feelings are that every man and woman who will not obey this counsel shall be severed from the Church, and let all who feel as I do lift up the right hand. [The vote was unanimous.] That is a pretty good vote.*[6]

Economic idealism had been exercised in limited form in the Perpetual Emigration Fund activities and the Public Work projects. The system where self-seeking individualism and personal aggrandizement would be completely replaced by common action, simplicity in consumption, relative equality, and group self-sufficiency—leading eventually to a more perfect society—came through a cooperative movement that led to reorganization of the whole Mormon society. The cooperative organizations came to be known as United Orders.

THE UNITED ORDER PROGRAM SOLUTION

During the years of 1873 and 1874, the United Order program was advocated. Many such organizations were started, though most did not last. However, their cooperative effects impacted Mormon manufacturing and merchandising well into the twentieth century. The United Order movement promoted thrift and made possible rapid accumulation of funds with which to buy equipment and machinery. It also assured more rapid development of resources in isolated areas that had disadvantages for successful colonization. An added advantage of the United Orders was the construction and furnishing of temples in Salt Lake City, St. George, Logan, and Manti, which required the cooperative efforts of the finest Mormon carpenters, cabinetmakers, and chair makers.[7] (figures 1.6, 3.35)

Mormons lived in all different types of communal "orders." Furniture, among other products of necessity, was made by and for people who sought to become self-sufficient. Four kinds of orders can be defined:

1. The first was an order in which the people contributed all of their economic property to the order and received differential wages and dividends, depending upon their labor and the value of the property they contributed. Gains were achieved through the increased specialization of labor and by cooperative farming. Half of these orders lasted no more than a year.

2. The second was an order that reinforced and extended the cooperative business network already in existence and did not require the giving of all one's property or labor to the group. It relied instead upon a contemplated increase in community ownership and operation of cooperative enterprises. The community ownership and operation of sawmills, lath and shingle mills, blacksmith shops, tanneries, boot and shoe shops, cabinet and furniture shops, millenaries, sheep and dairy herds, and creameries, was most successful in Brigham City and Hyrum in Utah, and in Paris, Idaho.

3. The third type of order occurred in many of the Latter-day Saint wards in the largest cities, such as Salt Lake City, Ogden, Provo, and Logan. These groups utilized a modification of the second kind of order. In their approach, a single cooperative was organized in each ward to promote some needed enterprise. Even though there was little opportunity for cooperative labor, surplus capital was mobilized to provide employment and to develop the territory. Many of these orders lasted into the 1880s, but most continued operation under private auspices. (figure 4.18)

4. The fourth type of order was a communal plan which called for groups of 50 to 750 settlers to contribute all of their property to the community. Holding no private property, they shared more or less equally, dressed similarly, and lived and ate together as a well-regulated family. They were directed by a Board of Management, and their life was regulated by a United Order bugler who signaled the community to rise, to eat, to attend to prayers, to go to work, and to return from work. These communities achieved a remarkable degree of self-sufficiency. Orderville is the best-known example, but other orders functioned effectively in Price City, Springdale, and Kingston, Utah. Bunkerville, Nevada, and other communities of

FIGURE 4.18

HIGH-BACK CHAIR
Anonymous maker
Name incised in back: Bishop Winder
Red pine
41 x 22 in.
Seat height: 17 in.
Collection of Richard Blanck

northern Arizona had successful cooperative orders as well. Most continued until the anti-polygamy persecutions of the 1880s.

Workshops in those orders varied according to the need for equipment and materials to supply them. Many orders displayed their merchandise in the central storehouses, while others showed theirs in large cooperative stores. Exchange and distribution varied by region. The furniture of Orderville has been found all over southern Utah; pieces produced in Brigham City supplied homes in Cache, Box Elder, Morgan, and Rich Counties. P.U.M.M.I. furniture supplied Iron, Washington, Beaver, and Garfield Counties.

Patterns for furniture design were established by the master cabinetmaker in each order. In some workshops, such as the Brigham City order, labor was shared to produce furniture pieces that had both English and Scandinavian characteristics. The individual pieces showed the diversity of people cooperating together to produce a unique style. The furniture design is unique to each order. The simple furniture produced in Orderville in the 1870s and 1880s was more like the simple furniture built by the first Great Salt Lake City settlers in the period of 1848 to 1855. It is apparent that the stages of settlement continued to influence style well past the initial colonization effort's first decade.

A clear example of diversity in design within a United Order furniture workshop is the Brigham City cupboard built primarily by Scandinavian cabinetmakers using English proportions. The cupboards were then grained by English painters and grainers. Brigham City style was also influenced by the railway supply center in nearby Corrine. Fashionable eastern and European furniture elements were incorporated with the details already in use by the United Order craftsmen. The eclectic design and finishing approaches of Mormon furniture throughout the settlements, but particularly in pieces created in United Order shops, evolved styles that can only be defined as Mormon. A more in-depth discussion of the contrasting orders of Orderville and Brigham City will clarify the interplay between cooperative effort and diversity of culture and taste.

ORDERVILLE UNITED ORDER

By 1877, the economy was not so precarious, and the necessity of group action for survival was not so immediate. The death of Brigham Young that same year removed the influence of the United Order's chief advocate. Most of the hundreds of order groups passed out of cooperative fashion. Because isolated communities such as Orderville and the Little Colorado River settlements in Arizona, Virgin River Valley communities in southern Utah, Cache Valley groups in northern Utah, and Bear Lake Valley groups in southern Idaho needed cooperative financing to progress, those orders lasted into the late 1880s.

The material culture that existed during the years of 1875–85 in the Orderville United Order is most important to understand for its legacy of stability and style.

Orderville was situated in an isolated but beautiful long valley on the Virgin River in Kane County, Utah. The location was extremely rugged and is near present-day Bryce and Zion Canyon National Parks. The settlement was founded for the express purpose of establishing a United Order community. The twenty-four original families numbered one hundred fifty people uniquely disciplined in the principle of cooperation. They had been selected from many Utah towns because they had already attempted to establish settlements in the 1860s to form the Muddy River colonies in northern Nevada on the Colorado River; Las Vegas is one of those settlements. The dual intentions of those early Mormon settlers was to raise cotton and maintain a stopping place for emigrants on their way to and from California. That effort was unsuccessful due to drought, insect infestation, flash floods, and disease. Many of those settlements have since been abandoned and are now covered by the waters of Lake Mead.

That group of United Order settlers was recalled from Nevada to Utah in 1870–71 to establish their order in Kane County, naming the new community Orderville. Once more, their spirit of cooperation and organized effort produced a new colony. Orderville was more successful. The United Order of Orderville was formally instituted in 1875 when all the real and personal property of the colonists was deeded to the community corporation. The property included: hundreds of acres of land, houses, cattle, horses, mules, hogs, sheep, chickens, machinery, sawmills, and provisions.

Each donor was given book credit for capital stock in the corporation according to the value of his contribution. It was agreed that stock did not entitle the owner to dividends or to any share of the corporation assets. All participants agreed that all property would belong "to the Lord," and that each would be a good steward over his time and the property left in his charge.

By cooperative labor, they built small house units with a common kitchen and dining hall in the center. The arrangement of the buildings formed a semi-fort around the town square. They also built a bakery,

tannery, schoolhouse, telegraph office, woolen factory, and garden house, plus dairy barns, sheep sheds, and shops for blacksmith, carpentry, cooper, and shoemaking businesses. The Orderville United Order operated gardens, orchards, three dairies, a cotton farm, poultry farms, a woolen mill, a steam-driven sawmill, and a water-powered gristmill. From all of these cooperative resources they made their own soap, brooms, hats, silk and cotton thread, leather products, clothing, and furniture. Self-sufficiency was almost completely attained. (figure 4.19)

Food was served in relays in the dining room, and women took turns performing kitchen chores. United Order midwives delivered the babies. There were artists, musicians, and teachers for cultural enrichment, and the order became so attractive that the population of Orderville swelled to 700.[8]

The furniture and carpentry workshop had a turning lathe and a scroll saw for fancy wood carving. Three craftsmen were recorded in Orderville: Warner Porter was the chief carpenter, and Heber Clayton and Isaac Carling were cabinetmakers. Carling made all kinds of furniture, including cupboards, tables, bedsteads, and chairs. Both Clayton and Carling had come to Utah as pioneer children from Nauvoo, Illinois. Clayton's father had been the English scribe and secretary to the presidents of the church, and Carling's father had been a wood carver whose work had helped complete the Nauvoo Temple.

Carling and Clayton had learned their trades and understanding of furniture style from the early settlements of Salt Lake City, Provo, and Fillmore. The predominant style of those communities was reminiscent of the earliest practical designs of settlement furniture, and it fit the goals of simplicity espoused by the United Order groups. Orderville furniture was made from white pine and cedar, painted with oxide red, black, and green. Local pigments were experimented with but commercial stains were also shipped to the order from Salt Lake City.[9] (figures 4.20, 4.21)

Orderville's need for capital funds was met by selling their excess furni-

ture, leather goods, and other products to other southern Utah communities. Identified as one of Utah's best primitive furniture styles, Orderville's simple furniture antiques can today be found in southern Utah, northern Arizona, and Nevada. The money earned by the order from the sale of furniture and other products bought additional land and equipment for the cooperative. The United Order of Orderville also furnished tar and labor for the construction of the St. George Temple and supported two members who helped erect the Manti Temple.[10] (figure 4.22)

Financial statements indicate that there was always a balance of credits over debits attesting to the remarkable discipline and self-restraint of these hardworking people. Almost every published report of life under the order speaks of it as the closest approximation to a well-ordered, supremely happy Christian life that it is possible to achieve in human society. Unfortunately, circumstances outside the community led to its ultimate collapse as a self-sustaining order.

Orderville had been founded in an atmosphere of poverty and only through cooperative effort were its members able to eat and dress better than they had in many years. The rich mines at nearby Silver Reef created a boom in profits for Orderville's neighbors who were able to buy imported

clothing, furniture, and other store commodities. The Saints in Orderville became "old fashioned," and the cooperative's young people were affected. They began to compare themselves unfavorably with their peers in other communities who had what they didn't have and could even acquire property of their own. The United Order came up with a solution to set aside a portion of each year's income to buy capital stock for maturing young people; but the solution came too late. Compounded by natural disasters which stretched the group's resources, and the enforcement of the Edmund

FIGURE 4.22

WINDSOR OXBOW CHAIR
Anonymous Orderville maker
Pine, painted
25 x 19 in.
Seat height: 15 in.
Collection of Orderville DUP

Tucker Act, which drove most polygamous leaders into hiding and caused some to spend time in prison, church authorities counseled dissolution of the order in 1885.

In an auction in which each man was permitted to use his credits to buy the property of the order, the common possessions of all were distributed among the hundred or more families who had remained to the last. Many of those families stayed on in the area after the dissolution of the United Order in Orderville. The names of the original founders are the family names of many present-day Orderville residents.

Some families who moved to Chihuahua, Mexico, during the 1890s to avoid persecution for polygamy, formed a United Order organization that closely resembled that of Orderville a decade earlier.

BRIGHAM CITY COOPERATIVE MERCANTILE AND MANUFACTURING COMPANY

The families selected to settle Brigham City in 1851 included skilled people in the following occupations: schoolteacher, mason, carpenter, blacksmith, cabinetmaker, shoemaker, and tradesmen who would insure the economic success of the community.

They constructed a fort, gristmill, sawmill, cabinet shop, and other businesses for colonization. By 1864, a great influx of Scandinavian immigrants created a tremendous need for expansion of goods and services. In 1864, presiding apostle Lorenzo Snow mobilized labor and capital to promote home industry and agriculture. He organized a mercantile cooperative in which many townspeople took shares. Profits made were paid in kind as dividends to investors. The Brigham City Cooperative was so successful that it became a model for other community groups. Within four years, the cooperative had accumulated sufficient funds to build a $10,000 tannery, and by 1870, the expanded Brigham City Cooperative Mercantile and Manufacturing Company founded a $35,000 water-powered woolen factory. Almost every conceivable product from molasses and furniture to brooms and hats was produced in one of its many workshops. In 1875 alone, the total of the cooperative's production was valued at $260,000, of which $100,000 was reported to have been reinvested in new cooperative enterprises.[11]

Homes were built for the poor and widows, with labor and food being made available for those called "tramps" in those days. The opportunities for trade and business shops were located on a twelve-acre square in the center of Brigham City. Construction enterprises included a shingle, lath and

FIGURE 4.23

FURNITURE COLLECTION
Anonymous makers from Brigham City
  Cooperative
Pine, painted and grained
Furniture from the Alma Compton Home
Collection of Museum of Brigham City

FIGURE 4.24

PEDESTAL TABLE
Anonymous maker from Brigham City
  Cooperative
Pine, painted and grained faux walnut
29 x 30 (diameter) in.
Collection of Museum of Brigham City
  Corporation

picket mill; three sawmills, including a steam-driven sawmill; adobe and brick shops; a blacksmith shop; a lime kiln; a furniture or cabinet shop making products from white pine; a two-story factory fitted with machinery for wood turning, planing, and moldings; and architecture, mason, carpentry, and painting departments. In 1874–75, these cooperative-run departments employed 46 people who built 46 homes, plastered 163 rooms and completed work valued at $21,000.[12]

On 25 October 1876, a reporter from the *Salt Lake Herald* wrote:

If the example of the inhabitants of this town [Brigham City] was more generally followed, Utah would be far more prosperous and her people better off. Our present suicidal policy of exporting raw materials and importing manufactured articles would be stopped, we would be far more independent of our sister states and territories; the financial panics of the east or west would not affect us; our people would all have good homes and enjoy more of the comforts of life than they can hope for under present regulations; and our children would stand a much better chance of receiving good educations and becoming useful members of society.[13]

Brigham City Cooperative officials attempted to provide suitable work for every person desiring employment. By 1874, approximately 250 people were employed in various departments. Wages were paid almost exclusively in the products made in those departments. One type of wage was a redeemable paper useful in exchange for various industrial and agricultural commodities as well as admission to concerts, plays, and other community productions.

FIGURE 4.25

BUREAU
Anonymous maker from Brigham City
    Cooperative, 1870s
Pine, grained
Victorian design elements
72 x 42 x 21 in.
Collection of Pioneer Trail State Park

For the purposes of material culture history, the establishment of a cooperative furniture shop occurred as the building's owner, Judge Smith, sold the shop to the cooperative. Tables, wardrobes, bureaus, cupboards, food safes, and lounges all made from white pine with the aid of ordinary bench tools formed the core products of a thriving industry. British and Scandinavian craftsmen worked side by side during the period of 1886–89. The manager of the shop was Martin L. Ensign, and his cooperative cabinetmaking group included: Elias Jensen, J. C. Nielsen, Nels Dedrickson, S. N. Lee, James Ingram, Otto Johnson. Ingram, Lee, and Jensen were skilled in turning. Danish brothers Andrew George and Christian Mathias Funk, as well as Scandinavians John L. Anderson, and Moroni Faulkner were painting and graining experts. Apprenticed to the cooperative cabinetmaking shop were: John H. Forsgren, Charles Squires, and Ricy H. Jones. The furniture produced by this group was an amazing blend of English and Scandinavian parts, design, and graining.[14] (figures 4.23, 4.24, 4.25, 4.26)

In 1879, when private businesses were emerging outside of the cooperative, Elias Jensen made an entrepreneurial business move in that manner himself. He established his own cabinet shop and furniture store. By the 1880s, other craftsmen made the transition from cabinetmakers to furniture-store owners, often selling imported furniture that had come by rail.[14]

Some makers did continue to produce original designs in hardwood lumber they were at last able to obtain from outside sources and bring in by railway. However, it was a natural extension of the Mormon's taste for fine craftsmanship in furniture and other material goods that led them to give up their softwood "make do" pieces for hardwood imports created in the latest fashions in the rest of the world by the turn of the century.

NOTES

1. Dr. Thomas Carter, *The Traditional Way of Life, Essays in Honor of Warren E. Roberts* (Indiana University Folklore Institute, 1989), Bloomington, Indiana, 40.

2. Jules David Prown, *Style As Evidence* (Winterthur Portfolio), 15:197–210.

3. Anders Swensen, Letter to family in Norway, 14 July 1877, *History of Anders Swensen*, Mt. Pleasant, *Sanpete County History*.

4. Hans O. Magleby, *Journal*, Hans O. Magleby Memorial Foundation.

5. Elaine Thatcher, *Utah Historical Quarterly*, 1988, 56:334–5.

6. Brigham Young, discourse of 8 October 1868,

7. Isaac Van Wagoner Carling, Biography, 1–4, Orderville Daughters of the Utah Pioneers, gift of granddaughter, Ruby S. Swapp.

8. M. A. Pendleton, *The Orderville United Order of Zion* (Utah Historical Quarterly,) vol. 7.

9. See note 7 above.

10. See note 8 above.

11. L. J. Arrington, *Cooperative Community in the North*, Brigham City.

12. See note 11 above.

13. *Salt Lake Herald*, 24 October 1876.

14. Box Elder County records.

15. See note 14 above.

FIGURE 4.26

CUPBOARD
Anonymous maker from Brigham City
    Cooperative
Pine, grained faux walnut
Finials typical of the cooperative
Hand-carved drawer pulls
96 x 48 x 20 in.
Collection of Pioneer Trail State Park

CHAPTER FIVE

Faux Painting and Graining Techniques

❈   ❈   ❈

Advice from Stephen Shepherd, an Expert in Nineteenth-Century Painting and Graining Techniques

Author's note: Stephen Shepherd is a unique contemporary expert on the methods, tools, and materials used in painting and graining furniture and architectural elements in the nineteenth century. For this book he has prepared examples showing the buildup from base coat to final varnish in creating the appearance of the various woods, trompe l'oeil effects, and stone marbling. He has prepared a step-by-step account of accomplishing the various faux graining effects. These techniques were used in the Mormon pioneer period and continue to be achieved by cabinetmakers and faux-painting experts today.

Mormon pioneer painting and graining expertise derived from two important factors that impacted fine furniture making from divergent sources. The first has been repeatedly expressed: pioneers had severely limited hardwood resources. Fortunately however, the second factor surmounted that challenge: Mormon immigrants and craftsmen came from cultures where richly painted finishes were popular, such as those favored in Scandinavia.

The Empire era, with its emphasis on architectural elements and their use in furniture, fostered reinterpretation of these styles in the softwoods readily available to early immigrant farmers and craftsmen. Woodworkers built their furniture from the conifers, with some locally available hardwoods used sparingly in furniture parts where strength was needed.

The softwoods—including lumber with knots—were used because the craftsmen planned that the surfaces would be painted and perhaps grained, so that the conifer's plain grains would be disguised.

Some craftsmen finished their own work, others had someone who specialized in the trade provide the painted finish. As a result, today we enjoy

FIGURE 5.1

Detail, table top (figure 4.12)
Anonymous maker
Pine, painted and grained faux
   crotch mahogany
Collection of John Told

Crotch mahogany

Curly maple

Mormon antiques with painted finishes varying from crude, primitive attempts at graining to sophisticated faux finishes that fool even the most-trained eye.

CREATING GRAINING

There are two main types of graining that were used by early craftsmen and are still used by experts today: additive and subtractive. Each type of graining requires that the base coat (the painting) be the lightest color of the finish desired. The darker coat (the graining) is then added over the base coat to imitate the grain desired.

Faux finishes such as oak and maple are subtractive: the graining coat, usually a pigment suspended in varnish, is applied completely over the base coat. Brushes, rollers, feathers, and combs are then used to remove some of the pigmented graining coat, giving the visual impression of wood grain.

Additive graining is achieved by painting the grain directly onto the base coat. This method requires pigment suspended in shellac. All of the graining is varnished to protect and finish the faux patterns created. A satin or semi-gloss varnish is used for hardwood effects, and gloss varnish is used to achieve graining that resembles marble.

Finishes such as rosewood, mahogany, and maple tend to have been the favorites of the earliest graining experts, while maple, oak, and walnut examples appeared later. The following brief overviews explain how Mormon pioneer craftsmen achieved the effects of hardwood and other preferred, natural building materials as surface treatments on local pine to give the illusion of high-style European furniture:

Maple: The base coat of maple, as well as oak and leather, was a light yellow color. A lighter base coat provided the brilliance that glows through the graining, enhancing the look of the false wood by creating artificial depth, a characteristic of genuine hardwood or marble. The graining was usually subtractive; however, the predominant grain patterns could be painted on using additive graining. Once the paint was dry, the surface was coated with a burnt umber varnish mixture and the grain made by lightly brushing away some of the pigmented varnish. Because burnt umber is a natural earth pigment, it was available to pioneers; commercial preparations are available today.

Curly-grain maple was made by brushing over the surface along the intended grain pattern while gently moving the brush back and forth. In nature, the curl in the wood is perpendicular to the grain of the wood.

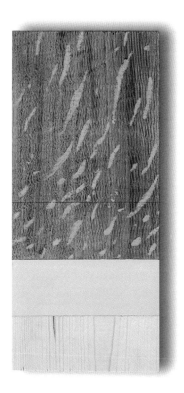

Flame-grain oak

Rosewood

Once the varnish graining dried, it was lightly sanded to make it smooth. Following the sanding step, the surface was sealed with a coat of varnish.

Oak: This is another hardwood effect created by the subtractive process. A light yellow base coat made of white pigment mixed with ochre pigment was used to create the appearance of oak. The base coat was always applied in the direction of the intended grain, which is not necessarily the direction of the grain of the pine onto which the faux grain was painted. After the base coat dried, it was sanded to a smooth finish and the graining coat was brushed onto the base coat.

The graining coat was burnt umber suspended in varnish. After the base coat was completely covered with pigmented varnish, spring-steel graining combs were brushed across the surface to scrape away the pigmented varnish wherever the teeth of the comb contacted the painted wood surface. The surfaces were combed twice in slightly different directions from each other. Curl was added by gently moving the comb from side to side as it was pulled along the surface. The flame grain of quarter-sawn white oak was put in by hand. Using the side of a finger or a textured roller that squeezed the graining coat from the base coat produced the characteristic flame grain. The furniture piece was then varnished for a permanent and protected finish.

Rosewood: The finest examples of high-style furniture were given the elegant rosewood finish. The base coat was a mixture of red iron oxide, or occasionally red lead, and a binder to form the opaque base coat for rosewood. It was also the method used to achieve faux mahogany graining. The additive graining coat was a mixture of black iron oxide or lamp black added to either varnish or shellac for the vehicle. It was applied using a dry-brush technique. The black graining was much sharper than the technique used for mahogany, which required the use of burnt umber as the pigment. Because rosewood tended to have a straight grain pattern, some artistic license was used in pioneer times.

Most examples from that period have the arched graining of slab-cut lumber rather than the common quarter-cut lumber. Very fine grain was added between the darker stripes with either a dry-brush technique or by using a checker roller. This tool consisted of a number of metal washers on a shaft with smaller washers in between for spacing. The larger washers were notched and, when coated with the pigmented finish, were then rolled over the surface in the direction of the grain, depositing fine, dark grain lines to the finish for very convincing results. The surface was allowed to dry and then varnished for protection and glow.

Mahogany: This technique—to achieve the appearance of mahogany's

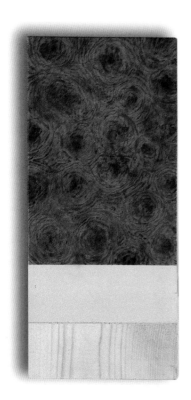

Maple burl

Walnut

interlocking grain, fine curls, and exquisite crotch graining—is described by most authorities as the finest work done by the pioneer craftsmen. Their properly executed mahogany graining often fools wood experts today. The brilliance of the reddish-orange base coat made of red iron oxide, red lead, or vermilion pigment, glows warmly through the burnt-umber graining coat. More flowing and less distinct than rosewood, all of the graining in mahogany is softer and blends gradually from darker to lighter areas.

Familiarity with genuine wood grain allowed the pioneer craftsman to imitate the unique characteristics of mahogany accurately. But as with most painting and graining, exact mahogany duplication with faux techniques was difficult to achieve believably. Brushes were used to apply the graining coat in an additive technique, although the subtractive process with dry brush, rags, or sponges was used to add additional effects. A checker roller filled in fine grain, and the whole surface of the furniture piece was then varnished with convincing results.

Maple burl: The base was prepared and painted with a coat of light yellow paint. When re-creating the intricate circular patterns of the grain that genuine burls have, a rolled-up square piece of cloth was used. Rolled into a tube, the end was dipped into the pigmented varnish or shellac and touched to the surface. The cloth roll was turned as it was touched to the base coat. This stamping pattern re-created the burls very effectively. After the initial phase was dry, the grain was dry-brush painted in between the stamping to copy the burl correctly. Some areas were darker than others, especially at the burls themselves.

In nature, burl wood is an attempt by the tree to heal damage to itself by forming small growth buds over and over in a tight pattern. Natural burls are unstable. They are usually cut into thin sheets to become veneers applied to furniture in fancy applications. Painted burls are also used in a similar manner. Although rarely found on antique, painted furniture, they do occasionally appear on finer pieces.

Walnut: This graining appeared on pieces of furniture and architectural details. The base coat was a light yellow to yellow orange color. Darker graining coats of burnt umber and shellac produced the overall grain patterns. Then a graining coat of burnt umber, with some black iron oxide added to the varnish, was applied over the entire surface.

Before the varnish dried, steel graining combs were drawn across the surface. By slightly moving the combs back and forth as they were drawn over the surface, the curly- or striped-grain patterns of quarter-sawn walnut were produced. Additional treatment could be done after the varnish was

Leather

Trompe l'oeil

dry by using a pigment of black iron oxide or lamp black in a vehicle of either slow-drying varnish or quick-drying shellac applied with a checker roller. This technique re-created the very fine-pore grain of natural walnut. As with all graining, the work was slightly exaggerated or enhanced to be more convincing. The lighter undercoat and layers of graining all contributed to the illusion of natural walnut.

Leather: Like oak, walnut, and maple, leather faux effects began with a light yellow base coat. Painted on pine, it was necessary to apply the base coat in two directions to give texture to the finished leather. On several older examples, the leather effect was painted onto coarse canvas which had been previously glued in a slight recess within the writing area of the piece of furniture, ordinarily some style of desk. The texture of the canvas contributed to the appearance of genuine leather.

The canvas was heavily coated with the base color to fill in the deep recesses, then was lightly sanded to smooth the base. The graining was done with burnt umber in shellac or varnish applied to the base coat with a rolled-up cloth or sponge. It was applied heavily to the edges and very lightly to the center. Some veining was added to copy the look of leather. After the graining coat dried, it was lightly sanded to remove the darker material only on the high spots to create the stippled look of authentic leather.

Several coats of varnish were applied to achieve the visual impression of leather, and then light sanding between coats provided a smooth surface for writing. The final coat of semi-gloss varnish worked to achieve the believable appearance of genuine leather.

Trompe l'oeil: French for painting that "fools the eye," trompe l'oeil has been used for centuries and in today's resurgent use is most often noted in architectural details such as moldings, crowns, and chair rails. It is occasionally found on mantels, on larger pieces of furniture, and as elements on finer furniture pieces. In pioneer times, it was perfected to an art form. Moldings were painted and grained to appear more like the material being copied, then shaded or shadowed to add a three-dimensional appearance. Hardwood architectural relief and furniture naturally darkens in recessed areas. By deliberately painting those ordinarily shadowed areas, the viewer is suitably convinced they are looking at genuine carved-hardwood relief. The idea was to create more detail than actually existed. By adding darker or lighter glazes of thinly tinted varnish or shellac, highlights and shading contributed to the illusion of relief. Even the cross-banding on antique tabletops or around fancy, grained panels exemplifies the degree of sophistication of which

Marble

the pioneers were capable and that skilled, reproduction-furniture makers achieve today.

Relatively plain pieces of furniture were transformed by Mormon pioneer artisans into high-style examples of the most dramatic furniture, whether European or Scandinavian in inspiration, through the use of graining and trompe l'oeil. By darkening painted joints between faux veneer, cross-beading, and in corners, the appearance of deeper details in moldings and carvings contributed effectively to the illusion of authentic materials.

Marble: Painted marble appears throughout the pioneer period as architectural elements, details on mantelpieces, and as all or part of the embellishments on furniture. The base coat was always the lightest color, as with all graining; however, other colors than white were selected as base coats. Light or pale green marble was often created with a bright peach color as its base coat. One unusual technique called for many bright colors to be applied in different areas with undefined edges covering most of the base coat. A thin wash of the finished color was then applied over the entire surface. The wash was ordinarily made of a varnish with pigment selected to match the final desired color. Several washes were necessary, and the more coats the better to help create the illusion of depth. The patches of different colors underneath the wash showed through in subtle shades to produce the illusion of quarried marble. Veining was added over the top of the wash to create the natural veining in genuine marble. As with natural marble, the faux techniques used to create veining and cracking tend to have one sharp edge, while the other edge was less distinct to appear as if it receded into the stone. A high-gloss varnish completed the faux marbling.

The various painting and graining techniques explained here were achieved to such a high degree of craftsmanship in the Mormon pioneer period, that the furniture preserved with these unique surface treatments astonishes historians and challenges today's reproduction-furniture makers.

FIGURE 5.4

TOOLS FOR GRAINING

REPRODUCTION FURNITURE MAKERS

L. Dale Braithwaite	Dale Peel	Stephen Shepherd
1960 South 424 East	565 West Main Street	2006 McClelland
Orem, Utah 84058	Mt. Pleasant, Utah 84647	Salt Lake City, Utah 84105
telephone: 801-225-2659	telephone: 801-462-2887	telephone: 801-484-1212

Bibliography

Arrington, L. J., Fox, F. Y., May, D. L. *Building the City of God.* Salt Lake City, Utah: Deseret Book Co., 1976.

Arrington, L. J. "Cooperative Community in the North [In Brigham City, Utah]." *Utah Historical Quarterly*, Utah State Historical Society, 33 (1965).

Arrington, L. J. *Great Basin Kingdom.* Salt Lake City, Utah: University of Utah Press, 1993.

Dalton, Luella A. *History of Iron County Mission.* Parowan, Utah: Daughters of the Utah Pioneers.

Dixon, Madoline C. *Peteetneet Town, A History of Payson, Utah.* Provo, Utah: Press Publishing Ltd., 1974.

Longsdorf, Hilda M. *History of Mount Pleasant 1859-1939.* Provo, Utah: Community Press, 1989.

Morningstar, Connie *Early Utah Furniture.* Logan, Utah: Utah University Press, 1976.

Papanikolas, Helen *The Peoples of Utah.* Utah State Historical Society, 1981.

Pendleton, M. A. "The Orderville United Order of Zion." *Utah Historical Quarterly.* Utah State Historical Society, 7 (1939): 1–7.

Powell, Allan K. *Utah History Encyclopedia.* Salt Lake City: University of Utah Press, 1994.

Robinson, A. F. *History of Kane County.* Utah Printing Co., 1970.

Shaw, Minerva S. *Stories from Our Museum.* Weber County DUP.

Thatcher, Elaine "Some Chairs for My Family: Furniture in Nineteenth-Century Cache Valley." *Utah Historical Quarterly.* Utah State Historical Society, 56 (1988) 331.

Watson, Kaye C. *Watson Life Under the Horseshoe, A History of Spring City.* Salt Lake City, Utah: Publisher's Press, 1987.

Worthington, K. N., Greenhalgh, S. H., Chapman, F. J., *They Left a Record, A Comprehensive History of Nephi, Utah, 1851-1978.*

Index